IN SOCIAL
RELATIONSHIPS

IN SOCIAL RELATIONSHIPS

An introduction to the social psychology of
membership and intimacy

Alan Radley

OPEN UNIVERSITY PRESS
MILTON KEYNES · PHILADELPHIA

Open University Press
Celtic Court
22 Ballmoor
Buckingham MK18 1XW

and
1900 Frost Road, Suite 101
Bristol, PA 19007, USA

First Published 1991

British Library Cataloguing in Publication Data

Radley, Alan
  In social relationships: an introduction to the social psychology of membership
  and intimacy.
  1. Social psychology
  I. Title
  302
  ISBN 0–335–15197–3
  ISBN 0–335–15196–5 (pbk)

Library of Congress Cataloguing Data available

Typeset by Burns & Smith Limited
Printed in Great Britain by Biddles Limited, Guildford and Kings Lynn

For my daughters
Katie and Lisa

CONTENTS

ACKNOWLEDGEMENTS

The author and publisher are grateful to Michael Joseph Ltd and to Simon & Schuster for permission to quote from *The Golden Notebook* by Doris Lessing; to Farrar, Straus & Giroux Inc. for allowing reproduction of a section from *Carnal Knowledge* by Jules Feiffer; to Paul Willis for permission to quote from his chapter 'The Expressive Style of a Motorbike Culture', published in J. Benthall and T. Polhemus (eds.) *The Body as a Medium of Expression*, and to Penguin Books for permission to quote from *Anna Karenin* by L. Tolstoy (trans. Rosemary Edmonds).

PREFACE

This book is the result of my having taught, over a number of years, a course called 'Group Dynamics/Social Interaction'. At first I taught it in the way it reads; first the group dynamics and then the social interaction. I found, however, that there were things that students wanted to discuss about individuals in order to understand what happens in groups, so I changed the order. This, as one might guess, did not help matters. The problem was that group dynamics and social interaction were terms for different aspects of the same, constant flow of social life. To add to the difficulties, much of the psychological literature treated these two aspects as if they really were different things, when both the students and myself knew that this was not so. It was inevitable, therefore, that I began to work out how best to present ideas which did some justice to the belief that intimacy can thrive in the most formal of group situations; and that, when two people meet in a personal relationship, they bring with them something of the groups to which they have belonged. This belief that society is made by people, and that individuals are made by society, runs throughout the following pages.

This book is different from most other introductions to social psychology in that it makes liberal use of examples. I believe that this approach makes new ideas easier to grasp, and that it helps to show the range and variety of the questions to which students would like answers. Perhaps most important of all, an example of one's own provides a hold on an issue, a direction towards what is important, what ought to be explained. A good example of a social situation, a feeling or an exchange can provide the essence of what social psychology ought to be able to tell us about our everyday lives.

Unlike some introductory texts, I have not included a wealth of references to studies in group dynamics or in social interaction. The reason for this is that the book tries to make an argument about the kinds of explanation which our examples require. This does not mean that experiments are ignored in the text, but that they do not have pride of place just because they were carried out in a laboratory. Room is made for examples and formal findings, and I have used both as I see fit. My guideline here has been to show the reader how we might explain issues of membership and of intimacy. Coverage, for the sake of it, has been resolutely avoided.

Perhaps because I work in a department of social sciences, the book includes more sociology and anthropology than is normally found in an introduction to a topic in social psychology. These subjects, I have found, are like an oilstone on which the budding psychologist can sharpen up his or her ideas in order to be more critical and stretch the boundaries of thinking.

The breaking of traditional boundaries between topics, the use of example and the inclusion of other disciplines are intended to provide a more accessible and yet critical introduction to social relationships than is presently available to the student or interested lay person. That is the aim of this book.

It might be thought that an introductory book is one where the author needs least help and therefore needs to make few acknowledgements. In truth, a book such as this one draws upon many conversations which have occurred over the years, involving both colleagues and students. Indeed, the approach to this text owes something to the way in which my interests in psychology were first kindled by my teachers, Marie Jahoda and Laurie Thomas, when I was an undergraduate at Brunel University. I am also indebted to the late Don Bannister, to Miller Mair and to Phil Salmon for their encouragement to me in the use of examples in psychology (particularly my own). I must also thank my colleagues in the Department of Social Sciences at Loughborough for urging me each year (in spite of any protestations on my part) to teach the course which eventually spawned this book. And to the students who commented upon draft chapters, I owe a debt of gratitude.

Other acknowledgements are in order. I am grateful to the late May Steinhard for translating the papers of Gustav Ichheiser from the original German; to Cathy Ward for help with typing and, lastly, to my family for bearing with me during the times when this book came first.

1

INTRODUCTION: EXPLANATIONS AND ILLUSTRATIONS

This book is an introduction to the study of social interaction. By social interaction I mean the ways in which people form, maintain and change their relationships with each other. The pages to follow describe how social psychologists in particular, and social scientists in general, have tried to explain the fabric of everyday life. Some of the matters discussed are very ordinary indeed, such as the way that people start conversations or take their leave of each other. Occasionally the study of social interaction involves accounting for experiences which seem special or important; for example, why a person whom we have known for some time has become difficult to get along with. Even saying hello to them doesn't seem the same anymore. This can raise questions about whether it is they or we who have changed. The possible answers that people mull over in their minds can be many and varied. Let us take an illustration to bring this point into focus.

Since her neighbour went back to work, Mrs Brown has found her to be 'less friendly'. No longer does she have time to chat or to meet together with their children; Mrs White seems somehow different in herself. She dresses more formally, talks about people whom she has dealings with at her work, discusses politics with Mrs Brown's husband and (there can be no doubt of this) even stands and walks differently. All this is evidence of a new-found confidence. What makes matters worse is that Mr Brown seems to encourage Mrs White in her conversation, as if the two of them now have things in common. Mrs Brown resents this and shows it in her manner towards her husband and her neighbour when they are together. What really annoys her, however, is that Mrs White either does not notice this change in Mrs Brown's manner or, worse still, doesn't care . . .

This scenario is sufficient to illustrate some of the things that we shall be concerned with in this book. On the surface we see a change in a relationship between two women who have been friends. It is a change for the worse, in that the feelings they have for each other seem to have cooled, at least on the part of one of them. A first attempt at explaining this might include the fact that Mrs White has now got a job, so that the things which the two women had in common beforehand (looking after the home and children) no longer stand. Mrs White now spends her time with a different group of people doing different things, about which Mrs Brown knows little, if nothing at all. Perhaps social relationships depend in part upon people being in a common situation, or else having things to do in common? This could be why Mrs Brown feels that Mrs White has left the group of housewives to which they belong, in order to join a new group of people who have other interests, other priorities. Indeed, being part of a group of people with whom one spends time and sharing with them one's experiences and concerns all help to establish one's place in the world. That, at least, is what Mrs Brown is coming to think now that her neighbour shows that there are better ways to spend her day and, perhaps, more interesting people with whom to spend it. The change in their relationship could be explained, therefore, as simply a casualty of the progress of Mrs White's career through different social groups.

It would be reasonable to object, however, that there was more to this illustration than a change in Mrs White's group membership. What of Mrs Brown's own behaviour, especially in relation to her husband and Mrs White? Does this not smack of plain ordinary jealousy? Could it be that Mrs Brown sees in her husband's attentions to their neighbour an attraction which could have something to do with that rather elegant way of dressing, and what seem like affected mannerisms? If Mr Brown could only be less taken in by this, his wife thinks, could only see what she so plainly sees and if he would only realize that she too has need of conversation. What Mr Brown knows or does not know need not be imagined here, other than to note that the way Mrs Brown reacts to the situation described shows that these relationships matter to her. They matter for the simple reason that she has been married to Mr Brown for the last ten years and has shared her experiences of motherhood with Mrs White for the last six. These events are part of relationships with their own biographies. While individuals do have business with strangers and with passing acquaintances, much of their social life involves people whom they know, on whom they sometimes depend and with whom they share their feelings.

Finally, could Mrs Brown's situation be explained more directly in terms of her own reaction to it? If asked to comment, we could advise her that, if she could only see things differently, she might try to alter events by becoming a little more confident in her own manner towards her neighbour, while at the same time taking an interest in Mrs White's new job. This line of explanation puts the responsibility for the bad feeling on the coldness of Mrs Brown's response following her reaction to her neighbour's manner. If relationships are made and broken by the little things that people do – how they speak, how they frown or turn away – then we can understand this exchange in terms of Mrs Brown's sensitivity to Mrs White's manner and in terms of her failure to communicate her own feelings. From this perspective, the Brown–White scenario is a case of mistaken and mixed messages.

While these three accounts of the scenario are not theoretical explanations of social interaction (in the sense that social scientists use the term), they are nevertheless reasonable as starting points for grasping what is going on. What they show is that social life, even in its ordinary aspect, is no simple matter. For that reason we should not expect the explanations of social scientists to be simple either. This is not a plea to readers to accept, grudgingly, complicated theories put together with jargon. It is instead a suggestion that students of social science should beware of wanting simple answers to make the world of relationships open up for easy inspection.

The three explanations given above all have a plausible air about them; they are not untypical of what any of us might say about the situation if asked. I would want to go further and say that thinking about the group membership of the two women, about their long-term relationships and about the detail of their dealings with one another makes for the beginnings of a better account than taking any one by itself. This, it might be said, is hardly surprising, because the more one looks at a problem in all its diversity the more one sees of it.

However, my reason for including each of the three accounts is more specific. It is an important reason, and is the keystone to this introduction to studying social interaction. Each of the brief accounts given above depended upon the others to make its point. When we think of the work group which Mrs White has joined, we implicitly acknowledge a change in the organization of her daily life, in the frequency and in the importance of the contacts she makes. Similarly, when thinking of the relationship of Mr and Mrs Brown, our attention is drawn to the fact that they spend their day with different people, in different group situations; and, finally, the references to Mrs White's manner of walking and to her style of dress made sense because we know that what is being referred to here is a change in her group status, as well as a change in her relationship to her neighbours.

The starting point for this book is that the study of social behaviour best proceeds by recognizing that, in real life, groups, relationships and individual actions depend on one another. How people walk, talk and move depends on who they are with, and in what situation; how people gain or lose the confidence of their fellows depends, in part, upon what they say and do and how they say or do it. The study of social interaction must therefore include reference to how these things work out in practice. For that reason, we shall often make use of illustrations like the one about Mrs Brown and her neighbour. We need to see how the different aspects of interaction which social scientists have studied make sense when we stretch them on the rack of everyday experience.

The problem of social interaction

What is the problem of social interaction? This might seem like asking, what is the key to understanding human relationships? By problem, I do not mean the *answers* which we might have about our relationships with one another, but the *questions* which we ought to be asking ourselves. To pursue the metaphor, one cannot be sure one has the right key until one has located the lock. Facing students of social interaction is the challenge of knowing just what it is that they should be trying to explain. In fact, this challenge can easily go unnoticed for two reasons, each powerful in its own way.

The first one is that, as students, we know a great deal about relationships, for the simple reason that we all take part in social life. The special feature of this knowledge is what the philosopher of science, Michael Polanyi (1967), called its *tacit* dimension. It is knowing *how* to do things rather than knowing *about* them. Our own experiences of life and of other people make certain things important to us, so that, even if we cannot say precisely how or why we do what we do or feel what we feel, these experiences stand as touchstones to which we bring knowledge gained from books. This tacit knowledge forms the basis of the questions which students of social interaction ask, even if they cannot always put them easily into words. Why then is it powerful? In part, the answer to this lies in the simple fact that it is one's own experience which is reflected daily in one's dealings with other people; it is how life is for you. Because we are, so to speak, inside the relationships which make us what we are, it is sometimes difficult to stand aside from them in order to investigate and describe them. This can have the undesirable effect of turning what should be a fascinating study of social life into a review of common sense.

There is a second reason why students might not be aware of the challenge to specify the important questions to ask about relationships; social scientists do it for them. It might be argued that this is, after all, an essential part of the teacher's function. My point is that an introduction to this topic places an obligation on the author or teacher to help students ask these questions for themselves. Providing answers obtained from particular investigations can give the impression that the problems for study are already agreed upon, and are clearly understood. The arguments that will be made in the pages to follow show this to be a questionable and fragile conclusion to draw.

The field of social relationships can be divided into an examination of groups on the one hand, and of two people, of dyads, on the other. This distinction has tended to be drawn when researchers have needed to delineate their field and to justify their focus. When studying groups only, there is a need to say what is peculiar to the life of groups. Similarly, introducing social interaction, an author may draw attention to features of individuals, emphasizing the role of personal goals and meanings. The separation of group dynamics and social interaction is well recognized and established in the social sciences. That said, there is widespread recognition among social psychologists and sociologists that social life embraces both our personal and our group existence at the same time. While choosing to emphasize one of these alternatives, the student is often cautioned not to forget the other.

What is going on in this uneasy division of relationships into their group and personal facets? Why can't we separate them entirely and get on with two distinct lines of enquiry? Alternatively, why have social scientists not managed to integrate the two fields into one? One answer is that the division remains because *it expresses a fundamental tension about social life*. We are both individuals and group members at one time, and these two facets cannot be reduced one to the other; nor, by combining them, can we retain what is essential about their difference. For it is in this difference that the tension is to be found, a tension which lies at the base of many of the most engaging and lasting debates concerning the nature of social interaction. That is why, when we settle for explanations which focus upon either the individual or the group, we grasp not only a problem simplified but also a problem made too simple. The interesting questions appear when we are prepared to retain the duality, the double-sidedness of our social relationships.

This goes some way to explaining why this book refuses to draw a firm line between group and personal interaction. Let us return, once more, to everyday experience. In any group people do not only speak to all of the members at one time ('I say you lot, look what I've found!'). Often we speak to one another in the group, so that couples converse while others listen. Occasionally this can be very obvious, as when two people draw to one side or lower their voices in order not to be overheard by the others. This sets the scene for jealousy or for conspiracy. What the two people share may be their secret, so that we are looking at a dyad operating within a group. On a different basis, we can take the example of a student who comes to the tutor asking if he or she can hand an essay in late. While there may be only two people in the room, the fact that the tutor is a member of a group of staff who have agreed to have rules about essay times makes the relationship more than just the meeting of this individual student and this individual tutor. We can see in these two examples that, while social scientists might agree to discuss either small groups or pairs of individuals, everyday life does not go along with this division of labour. In the course of our relationships we are sometimes couples alone and sometimes couples in groups; we sometimes act out our group life with many fellow members and sometimes with just one other person. This is one form of the ambiguity in social life to which we shall pay special attention in this book.

The sociologist Georg Simmel drew a further distinction between the dyad and the group of three or more people. Simmel (1965) argued that the couple is different because it is not a separate unity apart from the experience of its participants. If the two of them stop meeting, then the dyad is gone. In contrast, if one person leaves the group it remains; the group seemingly has a suprapersonal life. When two people are joined by a third party, the personal closeness may be destroyed. Something radical alters. Then two who speak are heard by another, for whom they become the objects of attention. Their relationship changes because it is objectified in the eyes of the third person. For this reason Simmel saw the dyad and the group as having special qualities. The lesson here is that we should not try to build a social psychology of group life out of the building bricks of two-person interactions.

The themes of this book

What follows is not a review of the *whole* field of social interaction, nor is it a summary of all of the main findings to do with the social psychology of groups and relationships. It is more of an argument about what I consider to be the important issues in the study of this subject. From what has been said about the use of examples in the text, it should not come as a surprise to know that I shall encourage the reader to draw upon his or her own experience. This is not the usual case in psychology texts which focus upon the literature (i.e. what has been found out already). I have always felt that one of the most restricting forces on students' thinking is their unwillingness to risk taking up explanations and then match them to different examples of real life. For this their teachers must take responsibility. Many a minitheory in psychology or a notion tied to a simple measure has been spared the cold blast of criticism which it deserves because the student has allowed it to rest on the particular case where it was first conceived. Those who assume that we are trying to replace common sense with science might think this approach inadvisable. However, their objective is one that I do not share. This book is a demonstration of and an encouragement in how to think about how people interact; it does not seek to substitute either theory or experimental findings in place of the reader's own experience. I believe that this is worth saying at the outset, so that the reader knows what kind of party it is to which the author is issuing an invitation.

This now brings us to the major themes of this book. The first is that social interaction *is essentially both social and involves bodily conduct*. By this I mean something rather everyday and something rather special. The everyday thing is that whatever we say or do together involves us both as members of the groups to which we belong and as people who express themselves with their bodies. The special thing is that we are, in our being, at one time both social and embodied creatures. An example drawn from my own experience will help to make this clearer. Once, looking out of the window from the train which had stopped at a station, I saw a family saying their farewells to one of their number, a young man who was finishing his leave from the army. He was with his wife and their children, and they were accompanied by what appeared to be either his or his wife's brother and family. The farewells were drawn out and clearly heartfelt, with the wife hugging her husband, while the children were held by the in-laws. The emotional scene was immediately obvious in the tears and clinging of the husband and wife, but also in the way that the in-laws held themselves away from this, while looking after the couple's two young children. Their consideration, the space that they gave the couple to say goodbye, while at the same time diverting the attention of the children, contained the emotional farewell as well as giving it a poignancy for the onlooker from the train.

One can see in this example of an everyday situation, both of the meanings to which I have drawn attention above. Here were people who indeed formed a group; the bonds of their membership were revealed in the pain of parting of one of their number. The hugs and the kisses of the husband and wife were the direct expression of this. To say that they were the evidence for it, or clues about it, would be to sell the encounter of the couple short. Neither group nor individual behaviour alone is satisfactorily made primary and the other secondary. We are faced with the prospect of having to acknowledge that people are both social and embodied (there is no better word for it) at once. More than this, I shall argue that acting socially (for example, taking part in group activities) always involves us bodily. Sometimes this is obvious, as when playing in a football team or being part of a dance troupe. At other times this occurs in a more subtle way, such as when somebody helps an old person across a street or looks after a sister's children while she says goodbye to her husband.

Let us briefly examine the second theme which runs through each of the following chapters. In the example above I said that the encounter was made more poignant for me, a detached observer, by the way that the couple's family, in caring for the children, both allowed the husband and wife to express themselves, and yet diverted the children's emotions which threatened to overwhelm the situation. There is here, I believe, something very important about human relationships. Through the judicious use of control, feelings are allowed to flower. By the spontaneous expression of feeling, the ties which bind people to each other, even when they are apart for many months, are strengthened. This important feature can be termed *an essential ambiguity in social relationships*. It is discernible in different forms and at different levels of communication. It is possible that it can be traced back to our first theme, in the duality of people's existence as both social and as embodied beings. However, what is important, at this stage, is to recognize that the decision to use everyday examples to introduce the study of social interaction promises to serve us well. Only by being prepared to outline examples in detail, and to bear with what may seem at times to be trivial particulars, can we see human relationships in a way that allows for the ambiguities we should acknowledge and explain. If this introductory text has a particular value, to lay person and student alike, it is to recommend that they bear this issue in mind as being important for a full understanding of social interaction.

2

APPEARANCES, CLAIMS
AND SECRETS

Some readers may have completed psychological tests which are designed to measure personality differences. Others might have filled in questionnaires in magazines or newspapers which claim to do much the same thing. There is something mysterious and exciting about the prospect of finding out what kind of person you are, remembering, of course, that these tests rarely, if ever, tell us all about ourselves. Perhaps this is the reason why they are so inviting – that they offer the opportunity to see oneself compared with other people in ways which one knows do not reveal the 'real' you. If, having obtained the results of one of these tests, people are asked 'Is that what you are really like?', most, I imagine, would say that, even if the description given of them is true in parts, it does not capture their personality in its entirety. There are several reasons why this should be the case, many of them of direct interest to psychologists studying how people make judgements about themselves and other people. One of the reasons often given is that what people are like depends upon who they are with at the time. Their personality appears to be different depending upon whether they are with people whom they know well, or with relative strangers. Appears to be different to whom? Well, our imaginary testee might say, 'I act differently when I'm with my mother than when I'm with my boyfriend; I'm different in myself, and they each see a different side of me.' For example, personality tests that tell the person she is 'introverted' might be rejected because the person in question insists that she is 'very outgoing' when with her friends. How we appear as individuals depends upon situations in which we do different things, and upon the views of other people to whom we mean something particular, or special.

I have begun this chapter with the example of the personality test because it brings straight to our attention two associated ideas. The first is that there is a difference between the judgement of personality as it has traditionally been studied by psychologists, and how people talk about themselves in everyday life. The second is that, when discussing how we are seen by other people, we make claims as to how we appear in their eyes and to the kind of people we 'really are'.

These two points are, in fact, tied together. On the one hand there is the picture obtained by psychological testing which claims to give an objective view of the person under consideration. On the other hand, there is the argument made by the individual concerned that this picture is incomplete. This incompleteness results not only from the fact that the test does not see what the person is capable of when with different people, but also from its failure to tap the knowledge which the person has about herself. The question of which picture is the accurate one becomes an argument as to what kinds of evidence will be taken into consideration, and whose claims to authenticity will be accepted. When we start talking about how people appear to each other in the course of their social relationships, we become involved in a discussion about claims as well as about perceptions, and engage in arguments about private as well as about public knowledge.

Visibility in social relationships

It is obvious that, when in face-to-face relationships, individuals are visible to one another. At the very simplest, one might say that all appearances depend upon this fact. What one person can see of another is the basis upon which first impressions, at least, will be formed. This is true, unless one has been given some information about the person beforehand. Having read books by particular authors one can form an impression of what they might look like, or how they might act when one meets them. This example of the author met first in type and only later in the flesh, was used by the Austrian sociologist Gustav Ichheiser (1949) in a lengthy paper discussing the problem of misunderstandings in human relations. His ideas were to have a considerable but, until recently, a largely unacknowledged effect upon the way social psychologists think about social perception (Boski and Rudmin 1989).

Ichheiser first made a distinction between 'expressions' and 'impressions', as these terms are used when talking about social relationships. 'Expressions' he termed those behaviours which come from 'inside' the person, such as emotions and impulses. 'Impressions' was the term which he reserved for the meaning which people place upon a person's behaviour from, as it were, the outside. Today this division would be found too simple for some social scientists. However, it serves to make an important point which, at the time that Ichheiser wrote, was not at all obvious and even now remains unclear to many. His argument was that the study of social perception, of the place of appearances in social relationships, is essentially a matter of the forming of 'impressions'. These are concerned not with personality as such, but with the *image* of personality. For example, to understand why two men always seem to be arguing we need to find out not what each is really like (in a psychological test sense), nor what each insists he means to say, but how the two of them interpret the other's communications. It was Ichheiser's contention that, because 'impressions' and 'expressions' cannot be reduced to one another, there will always be a difference between these two aspects of social life. Even when the two men in the example stop quarrelling there will remain a distinction between what each shows in his feelings and what the other makes of his behaviour. This does not mean that there will never be harmony between them; it does mean that where we see harmony we should not assume an exact correspondence between feelings and action, between 'expression' and 'impression'.

By focusing upon impressions Ichheiser drew attention to another distinction, which will be the focus of this section. He argued that all of our common-sense experience is perceivable either by the individual alone, or collectively by others. The first case includes our private experiences and feelings which, though we might communicate them to others, retain for us an aspect of the individual world of which they are part. The second case includes all those things about us which are perceivable by others, including our possessions, our physical presence and our actions. For Ichheiser, people have both individual ('socially invisible') and collective ('visible') aspects to their personalities. However, the socially 'visible' and 'invisible' aspects of personality are not completely separate regions. Aspects of the exchange can be sometimes private, sometimes public and sometimes both. There will be things which can be seen by both parties and things which can be seen (or experienced) by one only. At one extreme are our innermost feelings; at the other are objects, the things which we own and by which we are identified. Sometimes we want to express (in Ichheiser's sense) these inner feelings so that others can see them. At other times the reactions of other people to something publicly visible can make a person wish to hide it, such as when a visitor implies that an object in one's home is unsightly.

The regions of the 'visible' and the 'invisible' are not, however, clearly separated. There are thoughts and feelings which are, as it were, trying to be expressed, and there are actions and words which are simultaneously being modified to make them less open to scrutiny. The crucial point is that this ambiguity is not exceptional in social life, but commonplace. The following illustrations draw upon this important proposition.

Imagine a man and a woman who are eating out at a restaurant on a first date. Both, naturally enough, are concerned to make a good impression, for both want the relationship to develop. The woman wears a dress with a high collar, as she often does because she has what she believes to be an unsightly mole on her neck. In the course of helping her off with her coat, the waiter disengages the catch on the collar which falls open. The man sees the mole but remarks only upon the attractiveness of the dress. Here is an example in which visibility is dealt with at a literal level; a mole on the neck which was 'invisible' has become, if only for a moment, part of the collective 'visible' world. What is important is that the man sees the mole but acts as if

what Willi *really is*, is quite by the way? It is what he appears to be to the others at the table which matters to the reader, and I would argue, to the student of social relations.

Finally, it must be remembered that what Ichheiser has offered in the concept of visibility is a metaphor, not a literal description. In using the example of the woman with a mole on her neck, the explanation of the concept is made easier. However, a moment's thought will show that what was also disclosed was something about the man's feelings, something quite intangible and impossible to locate in the perceptual field. In fact, the use of the word 'perception' as applied to relationships is misleading, for the very reason that the student is led to believe that there are 'people things' to be seen with the eyes in much the same way that there are physical objects.

To summarize the argument so far, we can say that people's appearances are a function of both expressive and impressive features which operate together. There is no exact parallel between them, because they depend upon the individual and other people. Expressive acts or words do not simply emerge fully fledged from people's feelings for or about each other, nor do we gain direct impressions of other people's real personalities. As a result there is an uncertainty concerning our perceptions of each other which, in our social relationships, we can work either to clarify or to obscure. In saying this we are endorsing a fundamental shift in thinking about social relationships, a shift which Ichheiser first set in motion. Rather than assuming people's perceptions of each other to be a catalogue of mistakes and shortcomings (assuming that there are 'real' personalities to be seen), the argument can be turned on its head. Then one asks how people work with the ambiguities of social life in order to establish relatively stable personalities for themselves in their social relationships.

Appearances and realities in social life

Ichheiser (1949, 1970) put forward a simple, yet intriguing scheme for describing the way in which we know each other in everyday life. He suggested that this knowledge can be divided into three kinds, the 'real', the 'sham' and the 'pseudo'. I shall follow his procedure of placing quotation marks around these terms in order to draw attention to the special ways in which they are being used. Each of these words denotes a different way in which a person can be characterized, so that each one tends to give a different slant upon what we call the 'personalities' of people in social relationships.

'Real' characteristics are those which can be said to belong to people irrespective of the situation in which they are in. They have the stamp of an ability about them, such as being able to solve mathematical problems or play the piano or run a six-minute mile. Of course the possibility of actually doing any of these things depends upon the situation which the person is in, and upon other opportunities for their execution. Nevertheless, what

Ichheiser intended by this category was a personal quality which was demonstrable in ways relatively independent of the situation.

'Sham' characteristics are those which are credited to the person by other people. They have the status of attributions, and are more or less in agreement with how individuals actually think of themselves. So, for example, a man in a responsible social position might give the air of being a moral, upright individual. This characteristic is one which is, in fact, attributed to him by the people with whom he comes into professional contact, who can know little if anything of the way in which he conducts his personal life. For the man himself, giving the impression of being somebody who has high standards of morality is consistent with and supportive of his working role. It therefore suits him to accept the qualities which his clients lend to him and indeed may have come to expect from him over the years. In his actual dealings with colleagues and acquaintances, however, this man might show a lamentable shortfall in what these others have assumed him to be. It is in this sense that these qualities are 'sham' ones; they originate within the social system rather than the individual. However, they do not do so by chance, nor are they less tangible because of it. Taking up the example of our 'moral' person, it is in part because he holds a responsible position in society that he is so perceived. Ichheiser argues that, although 'sham' characteristics are often contrary to the ways in which the people concerned actually think of themselves, they should not be thought accidental. They are the product of stereotypes and attitudes which different groups of people hold about one another. This can explain why some people find that they cannot sustain the high expectations that others come to hold of them, knowing that they themselves have weaknesses which they acknowledge and accept. 'Sham' characteristics are, in a sense, double-edged; they provide a social current of opportunity along which each of us can allow ourselves to be taken, but they can also become a tide of obligation which will sweep us away from our own considered goals in life.

'Pseudo' characteristics belong to the most interesting class of Ichheiser's trio of categories. This term refers to qualities which people have as a direct consequence of occupying certain social positions, so that they appear to belong to them personally. They are not 'real' because, should the person lose the position, the characteristic is lost as well. So, for example, a politician seen as 'successful' and 'influential' may lose these qualities if he or she fails to be re-elected at the next election. More precisely, the politician can no longer *act as if* he or she were successful and influential. What distinguishes the 'pseudo' from the 'sham' is that, where the latter are attributions made by other people, the former are qualities or powers which are exercised by the individual concerned. 'Pseudo' characteristics are at the disposal of the person, enabling that individual to present himself (or herself) through the fabric of the social role which s/he occupies.

Ichheiser saw these qualities as very important in the way that people treat each other and express their own identities. For where the 'sham' characteristics are things which we may endorse (or at least, not oppose) in order to appear as others see us, 'pseudo' characteristics have the feel of being what we really are as social individuals. Depending upon the person's position, the teacher's 'wisdom', the doctor's 'good judgement', the businessman's 'enterprise' are qualities which they not only borrow, but lay claim to as being what they are as people. Individuals express these qualities in the course of their relationships with others, identifying themselves with them so much so that, should these features of their personality be challenged, they will feel piqued, if not sensing that their pride has been dented.

These three ways in which people appear to each other are not separate and unchanging. They interact in important ways to enable us to be the kind of personality that we might wish to be with other people. Ichheiser gives the example of a professor of mathematics who enjoys both a high academic reputation as a teacher and is renowned to be of high integrity. Unfortunately he enjoys gambling and one day loses money and signs a cheque which he cannot cover. He is dismissed from his post and remains redundant. We can identify his mathematical abilities as his 'real' characteristics, his qualities as a teacher as his 'pseudo' qualities and his reputation for being a reliable and honest man as his 'sham' qualities. As a result of his dismissal, his standing in the eyes of other people ('sham') may be irreparably damaged, so that he cannot take up a position (as a professor) which would enable him to show his ('pseudo') qualities as a teacher. If the situation continues for long enough, his mathematical ('real') skills may decline for want of use.

What Ichheiser most wanted to point out, however, was this. Features of personality which in everyday life we ascribe to people as essential parts of them as individuals are often not so at all. They are qualities which these people are allowed to claim as their own because of the position which they hold. We are not unfamiliar with this in everyday life, where it is well known that 'nothing breeds success like success'. 'Pseudo' characteristics *enable* people to act in ways that they otherwise could not, while all the while appearing as if they are part of the natural make-up of the person concerned. Indeed, because these characteristics form a large part of our social life, their importance is far greater than their label suggests.

Social psychologists have picked up this phenomenon in other forms. For some time it has been known that there is a tendency for people to generalize their knowledge of a person (the so-called halo effect), so that success in one arena would tend to credit the individual with the likelihood of success elsewhere (Schneider, Hastorf and Ellsworth 1979). In relation to the 'sham' characteristics, experimental work has shown the formative effect of an influential person's expectations upon others. As an illustration, it has been shown how expectations which teachers have of children are adopted by them as guidelines for their own academic aspirations (Rosenthal and Jacobsen 1966). That is to say, both 'sham' and 'pseudo' characteristics have real effects in people's lives. They are the basis of decisions about what one can and cannot do, what one can and cannot say.

'Can do': the scope of possible attainments

This section forms a bridge between the ideas of Ichheiser on the social psychology of appearances, and the theory of Erving Goffman about how we manage impressions in our relationships with others. Goffman, as we shall see, was concerned with how people claim particular 'selves' or identities in the course of interaction. However, in order for them to do so, it is arguable that people must have some sense of what they can do or can be. Appearances are not merely attributed, as it were, on to people; they are also the basis for our estimations of what we might achieve as individuals, both in the wider world and with the particular people whom we know well. These estimations have a basis in both our personal experience, by which I mean our thoughts about our own actions, and in the features of the social world which make them possible. These features, such as wealth and social position, are also the source of 'pseudo' and 'sham' characteristics. What is called a characteristic from the position of the perceiving person, is an ability, a 'can' (Ichheiser 1933) in the experience of the individual concerned. Appearances, therefore, are not passive labels but can be *enabling qualities*, adopted and then used by people to further their claims to be certain kinds of people, or else to live up (or down) to the 'sham' image of themselves which other people have fashioned for them.

There are two points to be made here. One is that 'sham' and 'pseudo' characteristics derive from aspects of people's social position. This is in spite of the fact that, once established, they appear to be *abilities* which are part of the personalities concerned. The second point is that, once taken on by individuals themselves, these qualities form the basis of what they feel they can or can't do in life – what Ichheiser called 'scope consciousness'. As an example, let us consider two men, of equal golfing ability, who wish to join the local golf club. One of the men is elected to membership of the club and so is enabled to improve his game and thereby his golfing abilities. The other man does not get elected and, being prevented from access to the golf course, is thereby hindered in his attempt to improve the standard of his game. Once elected and playing to a higher standard, the first man enjoys not only the satisfaction of being able to demonstrate his improved ability on the green every Saturday, but also the secondary benefits which will accrue to him as a result of being a club member. The fact that one 'can' play golf – in the restricted sense of skilfully using a club – is not the same as being 'a golfer', in the sense of occupying a position in the social world of golf. What Ichheiser was at pains to point out was that the social and technical means to improving ability (in this case membership of the golf club and access to its facilities) become assimilated in experience to the personal aspects. We regularly assume the credit which these aspects provide as belonging to ourselves, as individuals. Wealth, influence and social position are the main features of the social world through which people extend and elaborate their abilities. Once assimilated to our personalities they become qualities which we own as if we were born with them – good taste, authority and dignity.

The characteristics which people attribute to each other derive, in part, from the social groupings to which they belong. In cases where some groups are subordinate, or where people are denied access to resources enjoyed by members of other groups, the qualities attributed to them will tend to curtail or to diminish their sense of what they might do, or might be. Taken on as limits to 'oneself', these things are often in our conscious experience, not as 'can do', but as 'can't do' or 'won't try'. Here are some examples: the woman who won't ask for a drink at the bar, the man who won't engage a pretty girl in conversation, the student who won't speak in seminar discussions. For these people the social world is coloured by degrees of attainability in which male drinkers will leer, pretty girls will sneer and tutors (if not fellow students) will pour scorn on one's hard-worked thoughts. That is to say, our estimation of our own and of others' abilities enters into the appearance of the social world in which we live, so that it is peopled by individuals whom we approach with confidence, others whom we are wary of, and some whom we know will acquiesce to our charms or to our demands, depending upon what the case may be.

As we shall see in the next chapter, our abilities sometimes depend upon their being drawn out or realized with particular people. For example, a girl might say that she can dance well with one boy but not with another. The converse can also apply, as when a new acquaintance seems to make it possible to speak or to act in ways which somehow never emerge when we are with our old friends. These, it must be stressed, are not merely aspects of different individual personalities. There is always a temptation to attribute these feelings of 'can't' to the failings of the persons concerned, owing to the knowledge which we lack about the situation of the people involved. This is a mistake. The essence of this argument is that the social world into which we are born is well set up with patterned expectations relating to different groups or cultures. Part of their function is to express a measure of 'you can't' to members of other groupings. Even where intentions are of the highest, as with the efforts of workers engaged in rehabilitating blind people, appearances are busily fashioned from expectations. In certain institutes for the blind in the United States of America, the 'clients' were shown to be 'trained' to accept a dependent status. This was the result of their being involved in a learning programme which emphasized what blind people cannot expect to achieve (in a world of sighted people) rather than what they *can* achieve (Scott 1969).

Claims and uncertainties

The basic distinction with which we began this chapter separated out the expressiveness of a person from the impression which he or she is deemed to have made upon others. The preceding section has shown that these cannot be regarded as quite separate things, for the simple reason that individuals can try to make an impression in the eyes of other people, just as others form an impression of the person's intentions and abilities. In any event, however one tries to be a particular sort of person, whether it be confident, witty or bold, one's actions are open to the interpretation of the various other people whom one is with at the time. The sociologist Erving Goffman (1971) made a special study of the way in which people manage their impressions, including how they each portray their own particular personalities and also together convey a joint image of the kind of people they are.

Goffman's writings are among the most influential in sociology (and social psychology) in the last thirty years. He began with Ichheiser's distinction between 'expressions' and 'impressions', but immediately related the two by saying that

> The expressiveness of the individual (and therefore his capacity to give impressions) appear to involve two radically different kind of sign activity: the expression that he *gives*, and the expression that he *gives off*.
>
> (1971:14)

It is worth pausing at this point to take stock of what Goffman has offered us in this sentence. First, he proposes that the two basic features are related through the expressiveness of the person containing, metaphorically speaking, his or her capacity to make impressions. People do not merely express inner feelings but have the power to make (good or bad) impressions through their expressive behaviour. Dancing to music on the radio, waving from a car, shouting at a football match are all expressive actions, in the sense that they take account, to different degrees, of the impression that the behaviour has upon other people. The second point that Goffman makes is that expressiveness considered as impression-making has two aspects to it, so that people *give off* as well as *give* information about themselves. We are used to realizing this in situations where people are not quite as they wish to appear. This might be because of something they say but is more often because of the way it is said or the person's manner at the time. Then we speak of becoming uneasy or suspicious about such individuals, and this has the effect of heightening our attention to the way in which they are conducting their business with us. At times it is something that people are wearing that detracts from the standpoint which they take towards us. I remember an argument with a cinema manager who adopted a superior tone (I was a student at the time) but failed to be convincing, partly because he wore a dinner jacket heavily stained with the remains of what I took to be hastily eaten lunches. If people are to wear dinner jackets in order to give an air of formality and authority, then their clothes must be clean and proper if others are to be so impressed.

Goffman proposes that all of social life involves people in these kinds of expressive acts, in which the messages deliberately given as well as those given off are open for others to see. These actions (or words) have what

Goffman calls a 'promissary character' about them, by which he means that every time we enter a social situation we make a double claim. One aspect of this claim relates to ourselves, to the kind of person each of us is. When meeting people for the first time there is the possibility to try to be friendly, or knowledgeable, or proud, or any number of things. Of course, one can try to give this impression, but there is no guarantee that one will not give off certain information which will make it impossible to sustain one's intentions. Perhaps you will be caught out by a question, or cough and spill your drink on the floor, or have that embarrassing incident at work dragged up again by a colleague out to make jokes at your expense. Even if none of these things happen, the other people are forming their impressions of you, matching your words to your manner, bringing together what you have just said with what you said before. This is expressiveness in the service of first making and then sustaining a claim about the kind of person one is. It can be considered as a way of presenting oneself in everyday life, which is the basis of the book in which Goffman first put forward his ideas. There is, however, an important qualification which we need to recognize about this phrase which I will set out in a moment.

In the meanwhile, there is the matter of the second aspect, relating to these promissary acts. Alongside the claim which people make about themselves, their manner also demonstrates what can be called their 'definition of the situation'. For example, a man who enters someone's office and stands hesitantly by the door may not be trying to portray himself as diffident, but nevertheless expresses in his reserve the kind of work relationship between the two people in the room. What we commonly call reserve, or pushiness or formality are often descriptions of people's claims about themselves in particular situations. What they define is more than a character for themselves because their claim is to a scope of potential action in that setting. Someone who enters your home, throws down his coat, puts his feet on the coffee table and lights a cigarette expresses in those actions a view of himself, of you and of your possessions. What is 'given off' in this situation is a claim to what 'can' be done if he so chooses.

The above example is too extreme to illustrate properly what Goffman proposes about social relationships. Rather he is concerned to show that defining the situation and claiming a character for ourselves happen in all relationships, not just those in which we try hard to make a good impression. Consider buying a loaf of bread in a baker's shop. Here is a very simple exchange in which presenting oneself as a special kind of person is hardly the reason for its happening – you want to buy some bread! Further consideration will show, however, that there is a variety of ways in which we can ask for a loaf, in which the assistant can acknowledge our request and deal with the transaction. If we are polite and friendly in our manner, and then are dealt with in an abrupt and offhand manner, we feel slighted. It is not that we needed to claim that we are 'really nice people', but that we treated the assistant and the situation in a certain way and expected to be treated in a manner consistent with that claim. Goffman calls this exerting a *moral demand* about how one should be treated by others. By making a claim of a particular kind, people also give up claims to be treated in other ways. If I make a brief and formal request of someone, I cannot show my disappointment if they do not then enquire about the state of my health, or whether my holiday went well last weekend.

The core of Goffman's analysis lies in the distinction between expressions given and those given off. In order to claim to be a certain kind of person, we must arrange that the messages given off are not inconsistent with what we say explicitly. Indeed, it is in the realm of the given off, the facial expressions and general demeanour, that Goffman sees most scope for people to present themselves as having particular characters. While it might first appear that what is given is what is said in words, while what is given off is expressed in general conduct, this is not strictly true. If you think of times when you have wanted to impress people, how you have acted has been as deliberate as what you have said. Indeed, to the extent that we think that someone is trying to impress us, we do not take his or her general manner for granted. One must not forget that the definition of what is given and what is given off needs to be appreciated from the point of view of both the actor and the observers. It can be quite disconcerting (as once happened to me after a guest lecture) to have someone accuse you of contriving a manner which you felt you had spontaneously expressed. Then you are faced with the claim and counter-claim as to the balance of spontaneity and affectation in your performance. While this is perhaps more likely to happen to those foolish enough to give lectures, Goffman would argue that achieving this balance in a satisfactory way for all concerned makes the situation seem either more or less contrived.

Goffman's theory depends upon a comparison of real life with drama. He borrowed the language of the theatre to suggest that in the course of acting in social life we make *performances*. As a consequence of other people's accepting and endorsing our claims to be certain sorts of individuals, a particular definition of the situation is upheld, as part of which is the self or *character* which we come to have. Just as there is no absolute correspondence between expressions and impressions, so there is no absolute match between the performance which we give and the character which is communicated. I may go into an interview wanting to show my confidence and determination, but in comparison with the other candidates (whose performance I cannot see) I may appear to the selection panel as too single-minded and overbearing. The question, of course, remains as to which of these pictures is the true one. This is a key issue for Goffman and the source of considerable misunderstanding of his position.

Perhaps we should just pause for a moment to ask why it is necessary for us to be concerned with the niceties of Erving Goffman's theory. Many textbook introductions leave the student with the idea that social life is little more than an arena for impression management, in which individuals use the front of posture, clothing and social position in order to fashion the image which they desire to have in the eyes of other people. One can acknowledge that people will vary in the skill and therefore the success with which they do this, but nevertheless social life must then appear as a vast collusion in which we dupe each other. This is a parody of the explanation which Goffman offers and not surprisingly (and quite rightly) it is rejected by many students as unconvincing. What Goffman actually offers is a view of social life which is an elaboration of the ideas put forward by Ichheiser. We have seen that these ideas put in question the notion that there are ready-made personalities which interact and which are there to be 'perceived' (as you would see a bowl of cherries). To where does this lead us in terms of Goffman's theory?

In order to appreciate this point, one needs to get rid of the assumption that people always have characters or selves which they want to portray. Characters do not inevitably precede performances, but rather they emerge from them, as a result of the acceptance of or the challenge made to the claims which people put forward. If others act *as if* we have conveyed a particular impression, then we can take it that our claim to be treated in that way has been sustained. For example, I might enthuse about a piece of music which I enjoy, and about which I happen to be knowledgeable. As a consequence, the other people in the group assume my enthusiasm to mean that I am a 'music lover' and something of an expert. In the course of our conversations they might defer to me on matters to do with music and, if asked, I will do my best to keep up my end of our friendship through this interest. It is just possible that being regarded in this way will foster my musical interests, and this can only be helped by the fact that I now seem to have a special place in the group which I previously did not enjoy. This illustration shows that the character of music lover (which need hardly enter my thoughts about 'what sort of person I am') is a product of the relationship and not a determiner of it. To call me a music lover makes sense of the whole exchange in which I and my friends engage, endorsing my implicit claim to speak with authority about these matters, and crediting them in their turn with the good sense to listen and to accept what I have to say. Generalizing this to the idea of the person's *self*, Goffman said:

> A correctly staged and performed scene leads the audience to impute a self to a performed character, but his imputation – this self – is a *product* of a scene that comes off, and is not a *cause* of it. The self, then, as a performed character, is not an organic thing that has a specific location, whose fundamental fate is to be born, to mature, and to die; it is a dramatic effect arising diffusely from a scene that is presented, and the characteristic issue, the crucial concern, is whether it will be credited or discredited.

> (1971:245)

In the above quotation Goffman refers to characters being credited or discredited, because it follows that what people 'really are' is a matter of claims being endorsed, of a working consensus, if you like, about how people can act with one another. There is not a 'true self' inside each of us against which our words and actions are judged. Instead it is the consistency of our performances, particularly the consistency of what is given with what is given off, that others use to assess the legitimacy of our claims. Should I, in the course of talking about music, let slip that Ravel's 'Bolero' is the greatest piece of music ever written, then my friends might wonder whether I know as much about music as I first seemed to do.

The issue of appearance versus reality

Deception in social life is a special case, and it should not be used as a typical example of how people create impressions. It creates a picture of a social world in which people are sometimes 'themselves' (really), and at other times *poseurs* making false claims. If one thinks that the latter is the basic model for social interaction, then of course it cannot be true of all our relationships. But deception is rarely that simple. Even when people are putting on a front, there is always the possibility that this is their regular way of going about things. (This is like saying that the deceiver's ploys are really part of his or her personality.) Indeed, in a world of uncertainties, there may be good reason to 'put on a front' as a way of getting to know people. However, Goffman's point is that such fronts, as part of one's performance, and as the basis for the self which the others might credit you with being, are indeed part of the person and cannot be disowned in this way. An interchange between two students meeting at a college dance makes this point quite nicely:

SUSAN: This is the first time I've ever been to a college mixer.
SANDY: Me too. I hate them.
SUSAN: I hate them too.
SANDY: It's such a phony way of meeting people.
SUSAN: Everybody puts on an act.
SANDY: So, even if you meet somebody, you don't know who you're meeting.
SUSAN: Because you're meeting the act.
SANDY: That's right. Not the person.
SUSAN: I'm not sure I agree.
SANDY: With what?
SUSAN: With what you said.
SANDY: No, I don't either.
SUSAN: You don't agree with what you said?
SANDY: (*Cautious*) How do you feel about it?
SUSAN: I think people only like to think they're putting on an act, but it's not an act, it's really them. If they think it's an act they feel better because they think they can always change it.
SANDY: You mean they're kidding themselves because it's not really an act.
SUSAN: Yes, it is an act. But they're the act. The act is them.

SANDY: But if it's them, how can it be an act?
SUSAN: Because *they're* an act.

(from *Carnal Knowledge*, by Jules Feiffer, 1972)

Perhaps one also needs to make this point in the context of our relationships with friends or with our families. For it is in relation to these settings that students often feel that Goffman's theory suggests a palpable nonsense, that we are false when we know ourselves to be most 'ourselves'. First, it must be said that Goffman is not suggesting that performances are worked out beforehand or are executed in a self-conscious manner. What he does say, however, is that they must be *worked at*, or *dramatically realized*. We are not merely 'ourselves' with friends but enter into the spirit of the relationship in order to make it happen. We feel ourselves to be spontaneous because, among other things, the self which we claim is one which we can elaborate with a high certainty that it will be endorsed by our friends. Nevertheless, one must still make an effort (fashion a performance) even with friends and family. Go to the pub but refuse a drink, and then sit in quiet agreement with what is being said. You may not be a dissenter from the conversation but you are likely to be accused of being a 'wet blanket'. Even in their own home people are expected to maintain a degree of interest and participation in what is going on around them. Should they fail to do so, somebody in the family is likely to ask, 'What's the matter with you today?'

Dramatic realization is not a false playing-up of our social roles but a way of making them convincing and real. In the world of work people are expected to adopt a businesslike manner, not just for appearance's sake but because this sustains the claim which everyone involved endorses about 'the kind of firm we work for'. In the world of romance, being a lover has to be worked at too. It is not enough to *give* the message 'I love you', but one must *give off* the sentiment in one's manner. One does not have to be a social psychologist to understand why the transformed Eliza Doolittle in *My Fair Lady* sings to her diffident suitor, 'Don't talk of stars shining above, if you're in love, show me!' To play a particular role or to be a valued member of a group depends upon more than just possessing the 'right personality'; life has to be lived, we have to make something of our relationships if we are to make more of ourselves.

Deception, on the other hand, is something special because we begin with the separation of real self from false action. Even where this happens, it can have unexpected consequences, because appearances have real effects. Imagine a middle-aged lady with little experience of men but a considerable bank balance. Now imagine a young man of few scruples who decides to part the lady from her money. He charms her, takes her to Paris for an extended holiday and spends as much of her money as he can: then he leaves her and goes away. Her friends sympathize and tell her how badly she has been treated, and how awful all this must seem. To their amazement, she retorts that she has never had such a good time in her life and she intends to do more of this kind of thing in the future. Now this might be an unlikely story, but it is a possible one and goes to show how the determination by one person to control a relationship can lead to consequences which he or she never anticipated. Like the woman in the story, we form and reform impressions, not only of the other person, but also of ourselves. This means that our claims to what we cannot do or cannot be are also open to reinterpretation.

The gap between expression and impression, between what is visible to one person and not to another, between what is given and given off, is testimony to the ambiguity in human relationships to which attention has been drawn. The uncertainties in our dealings with each other are an essential part of the potential arising from the claims and the counter-claims of our performances. If we take this position, these uncertainties and contradictions are misunderstood if we see them arising from some ideal goal of accurate perception, perfect expression, and absolute control of the situation. And yet these assumptions have often lain beneath psychological studies of social interaction attempting to discover what, exactly, causes people to act as they do in their dealings with one another. This has left their authors with the problem of what to do about such things as pretence, charm, humour and sarcasm which depend upon appearances for their purposes, and which form an important part of our everyday experience.

Secrets and saying only so much

If we show only part of ourselves to different people in different situations, then it is inevitable that there will be aspects of ourselves which are known to some and hidden to others. To one's parents are shown certain behaviours which are kept from one's friends, and vice versa. Everybody is familiar with this situation and the idea of the multi-faceted person is now commonplace in Western societies. In this section I want to take up this topic in relation to the issue of secrecy in social relationships. Having done that, I hope to show that the idea of the many-sided individual is, if not a false one, then at least an inadequate one for social psychology. We are not ready-made objects to be viewed first from this side, then from that side, with the different parts retaining their form as the eye of the beholder scans and then passes by.

We have already seen that knowing someone involves attention both to what they say (give) and to their general demeanour (give off). What a person conveys is a claim to be a certain sort of person *and thereby to be not another kind of person*. This claim is dramatically realized, in Goffman's terms, through actions which put forward certain features and, necessarily, withhold others. If you are to show interest in what another person is saying, you must not look away or at other people during times in the conversation when you understand only too well, or when you are not too sure what is being explained. Those moments of boredom and of puzzlement are kept to oneself, either for reasons of good manners or in order to keep up appearances. They are unvoiced experiences, although the other person might discern something from our expression which suggests that he is in fact boring us. Whether he wishes to say at that point 'Look here, am I boring you?' is another matter, for it might not be in his interest to risk us saying, if not in so many words, 'Actually, you are, and I can't stand it a moment longer!' Better to change the topic of conversation and try to rescue the meeting.

The above example reveals that, far from seeing a completed and stable 'side' of a person's personality, we are engaged in a continuing (but often non-conscious) process of matching claim against possibility. What is unsaid can be as important a reckoning in our judgement as what has been said explicitly. We only say so much because to say more would be incompatible with our claims both to be who we are and to our view of the other person. Of course, there are times and there are relationships in which people put into words feelings and thoughts which they would not express to others. Family, friends and lovers are special confidants, although it must be said straight away that these relationships often do not overlap. Things said between lovers are not for the ears of one's parents or one's mutual friends, and this often goes for the other relationships as well. What is important is when we signal to the other person that what we are about to tell them is something which we would not tell to others, and which we would not expect them to divulge in their turn. Saying this, putting this gloss on the words, makes the exchange into a secret, which is not the same thing as information which one simply chooses not to put into words. More important than reporting the bare words which have been told is revealing that they have been said, by one person to another. The limitations which we place upon the words we say are extremely important in helping to fashion the kinds of relationships which we have with other people, and the boundaries of the groups and the cliques to which we belong.

Having secrets is commonplace and does not carry social comment or censure, except in relationships where there is an expectation that people should be open and honest with each other. In the market-place of society, however, this expectation certainly does not hold, owing to the assumption that people must 'get by' in situations where their personal weaknesses may be irrelevant. Goffman mentions individuals for whom there are special dispensations concerning what they should be able to hide. Among his examples are the 'ex-convict, deflowered, epileptic and the racially impure' (1971:67), all people who may acceptably cover rather than accentuate the marks of their condition. Indeed, the repeated disclosure of what others might not, under normal circumstances, be expected to discover is itself a situation for condemning the revealer: 'You know I've got an old war wound, don't you?'

What is there to be seen and what is not put into words are therefore not separate parts of people which alternate in the flow of social exchanges. Our knowledge of each other is always balanced upon a varying combination of the two, in which the public face of a person is fashioned around information which is known by others but which is not used to challenge them directly. The widow who is believed to be having an affair with a younger man is the subject of village gossip, of which she is aware but to which she never responds. Her public face is that of someone who scorns the hypocrisy of those who greet her with politeness but talk about her behind her back. Her manner, her personality in the village are products of what has become an 'open secret' about her behaviour. There is no certainty that the information is, indeed, correct. Perhaps she is not having an affair with the young man in question; and yet, perhaps under the circumstances, she thinks, 'Why not?'

Just as others can use information which they find out about us, so we can arrange that this information is discovered rather than revealed. Goffman talks about the ways in which people manage their impressions. In this case, the situation is special because what is being revealed is not just the information, but our way of handling it. People who have a problem which they are ashamed to discuss, but for which they want another person's help, might arrange to fail or to falter in something innocuous; this failure is then justified by their situation. For example, the businessman whose colleagues notice his mistakes at work and extract from him the confession that his wife has left him may gain both their understanding and their respect for his determination to carry on as usual. Information which his pride made into a secret becomes, on revelation, evidence about his attitude to work. This, most likely, would not have occurred, if on the day after the event he had come into the office and declared 'I need sympathy and support. My wife has left me.' Bearing up under our troubles, hiding them from direct view while allowing them to be reflected through other activities, is to be credited with having a noble secret.

3

THE GROUP SETTING

This book tries to show how ideas about social relationships can throw light upon particular kinds of situations; hence the use of illustrations within the argument. An approach to the study of small groups which is consistent with this way of thinking was set out some years ago by a sociologist, George Homans (1951), in a book which was to become a minor classic in its field. Homans's approach to understanding group life is different to that used by social psychologists who almost invariably use the experimental method to study problems, often setting up temporary groups in the laboratory. He opted instead to work out a theory based upon a detailed reworking of the reports of other social scientists about a range of real-life groups. What was important to him was that his explanation should encompass the variety of different kinds of grouping in society. There is an immediate consequence of choosing to look at a range of real-life groups which the laboratory approach avoids: the environments, the settings in which the groups operate have to be taken into consideration. These are things which are placed outside consideration in experimental studies which set out to control for their effects in order that the experimenter can concentrate upon the variables chosen for study. For Homans, one of the key issues in group life was the need for the group to survive in its setting; satisfying the demands of the environment therefore became a central issue within his theory. What makes the group a particular entity is that it acts as a system. This means that its parts – its members, its rules, its products – are mutually interdependent. We are used to the idea that, if people like each other, then they are more likely to work towards a good outcome, and that the success of their enterprise might give them a stronger sense of group identity. In a different vein, where a group is left with the legacy of a bad decision, then it can be the source of disagreement which sets up a vicious circle of discontent among the group members.

The idea of a system is different from the assumption of single causes and effects because everything affects everything else, indirectly if not directly. In a group of people the actions of one individual will have greater or lesser effect depending upon his or her position and influence in the group. Whatever the case, each individual's actions are dependent upon those of the others in the context of the organization of the group. The way in which this occurs is accounted for by Homans in terms of what was (at the time he wrote) a relatively new concept: negative feedback. This was a term borrowed from the newly emerging science of information and control (cybernetics). It showed how systems can stabilize themselves in a given environment by monitoring their own output. The thermostat which regulates the temperature of the domestic hot-water supply is the usual example given. The importance of this idea for group life is arguably limited, but nevertheless important in that limited respect. We need only to keep in mind that what people do in a group has effects upon other people, and upon the setting in which the group exists, and that these effects must be taken into account.

There is one important implication of this 'systems' way of thinking which ought to be mentioned at this point, because it will recur later in the book during our discussions of social interaction. It is the issue of *control*. Once regarded as a system of interdependent parts, having mutual influences, there is no single aspect of the group which we can point to as being 'the cause' of everything else. For example, the leader cannot be sought out as *the* reason why the group acts in the way that it does, because that person too is influenced in what he or she does. Instead of thinking of the control of a group as being *by* individual persons, we need to see control being exercised *within* the group *through* the actions of its members. What the group does and how it operates cannot be reduced to the sum of the wills of its individual members, but is an expression (so to speak) of the organization which we call the group culture, or ethos.

We have already met the issue of control in human relationships when speaking of the way in which individuals 'manage' impressions, so as to meet, divert or subvert the expectations of other people. When talking in this way there was always a lingering possibility that we were trying to account for social life as if it could be reduced to the wills of individuals taken separately. As a counter to that assumption, it was pointed out that the claims which people made through their expressive behaviour take place within a context of expectations which have a distinctly social form. That is to say, that the 'sham' characteristics which we try to live up to are already there, channelled in the differences fashioned by history and current social debate. Implicit in this argument is the idea of the shaping of social behaviour by individuals certainly, but within relationships which cannot be explained by reference to individuals only. For this we need recourse to the study of groups. This does not mean a shift to a new subject: groups are people interacting. As Homans himself once said, groups are not so much *what* we study, but *where* we study what interests us.

Satisfying the environment: the external system

In this and in the following section I shall introduce Homans's way of conceptualizing small groups, with an eye to employing his ideas to account for ambiguities in social relationships. True to form, let us use an illustration, one familiar to many who have embarked upon a course at college or university. Imagine a group of students who have recently arrived at college in order to study social psychology. They find themselves allocated rooms in the same hall of residence, and meeting in tutorials and in practical classes. We can regard them as a group, in so far as they spend more time with each other than with other people at the college. The environment, by making demands upon these people in different ways, brings them together in the first place. There are physical constraints to do with the spatial organization of their rooms in the hall of residence. This makes it more likely that, on first arriving, some of them will meet, introduce themselves and perhaps go to eat their meals together. They might also arrange to walk over to the first lecture, to student registration and to the bookshop to see which texts they ought to purchase. There are also technical constraints, involving the kind of work which they are expected to do. Technical aspects of the environment are most easily seen in relation to jobs done with tools, and the limitations (and opportunities) which these place upon the relationships which the person involved might form. Compare for a moment the social possibilities arising from using a road drill with those associated with using a camera. The one isolates the user in an envelope of noise which makes communication difficult, while the other produces a relationship in which the photographer must communicate with the model if a successful picture is to be taken. For the group of students, technical aspects of studying might involve time spent with books in the library (enveloped in quietness), as well as occasions when they must work together to devise and carry out a questionnaire investigation. The third aspect is one which arises from the social context in which the group operates. As students they are subject to the expectations of the college, of their teachers and of their parents and friends too. The organization of the teaching, the way in which lecturers set coursework, mark exams and give guidance are expressions of what Homans called the social aspect of the environment.

These aspects of the environment are reflected in the particular features of group life which Homans divides into *activity*, *sentiment* and *interaction*. Directed towards satisfying the demands of the environment, these elements make up what Homans calls the external system. This is a key concept which will be explained in the remainder of this section. 'Sentiment' refers to the wants, wishes, values and ideologies which people bring to the group as members of other groupings in society. All students want a degree; some feel that they need it more than others, for reasons of their own. Some students are hoping that college will bring the chance of making new and lasting friendships. The sentiments which people bring to the group are what we ordinarily recognize as the different attitudes or personalities upon which the relationships are based. 'Activities' are simply what people do in the course of being in the group, such as asking a question of a lecturer, writing an essay or making notes from a book. 'Interactions' are occasions when people are brought into relationship with one another, such as when students must work together in order to carry out an experiment during a practical class.

These features are themselves interdependent. For example, wanting to get a good degree (sentiment) might lead a particular student to speak a great deal during seminars (activity). This brings her into conversational relationship (interaction) with the tutor, who responds to her interest by suggesting some extra reading which she might do (activity). As a result of this reading she gets a high mark for her essay which goes to strengthen her goal of achieving a good degree (sentiment). This cycle of mutual reinforcement is not inevitable, although Homans sets out his theory in terms of a set of hypotheses which (he claims) supports the idea that frequency of contact strengthens sentiment, which itself forms the basis for further activity. Whether this is true on all occasions is not the issue at this point. Note instead that all three of these features relate to the job of being a student, to the educational process itself. Think of the group only in terms of its members wanting to get a degree, being required to write essays, attend seminars, and to discuss among themselves a topic which they have been asked to prepare. All of these things derive from the educational setting, from the environment which gives the group its reason for existence. The way in which these sentiments, activities and interactions begin to pattern themselves in the group constitute the external system. We might see certain individuals helping each other with essays, or working together on projects, or asking if they can borrow a book which one of them has taken out of the library. Sometimes these approaches and requests will be accepted or acceded to; at other times they will meet with a rebuff. Then there appears in the group a pattern of likings and dislikings which are attributable to individuals as persons, above and beyond the particulars of the matter in hand. It is important to note that the external system is the patterning of the behaviours and sentiments of the group as its members satisfy the demands of the environment. It does *not* refer to things outside the group (i.e. to the environment itself) but to a complete 'side' of the life of the group. The word 'complete' in the last sentence does not mean that these behaviours are closed off from the environment or do not change. It signals the wholeness or interdependence of the three features, so that we do not imagine them as quite separate responses.

The external system is, however, only one side of the group's existence. It is complemented by the internal system which refers to the sentiments, activities and interactions which arise out of the group's attempts to satisfy the tasks it must perform. We shall discuss this in detail in the next section. Before we do that, however, the idea of the external system raises some possibilities for the study of social relationships which we cannot allow to pass without comment. It suggests that all group life is based upon some relationship with a wider setting. This might seem obvious, were it not that a good proportion of social psychological studies of group dynamics has taken place without any consideration of this kind at all. This is not true of studies which have specifically examined the effect of the physical environment upon social interaction. It has been shown that how people are seated will affect the kind of relationship which they assume towards each other (Sommer 1965). It has also been found that the extent to which groups vary in both their effectiveness at problem solving and in their satisfaction with the task can be determined by the number of communication channels at their disposal (Leavitt 1951). Centralizing communications, putting one person in a position of co-ordinating authority can make a group quick at solving simple problems. By comparison, groups where individuals can talk to all or to most of the other members have been found to be slower on these tasks. Initially, it seemed that the judicious organization of the group's communication channels could determine productivity of decision making. In further studies, however, it was shown that, given enough time, groups which had not had their communication channels arranged for them would organize their own structure and become as efficient as the groups which began with a person in central control (Guetzkow and Simon 1955). There was the added bonus that the members of these self-organized groups did not suffer the variable levels of morale of the experimenter-organized groups. The lesson of these studies is that the environment and the external system are not to be confused. One cannot determine, absolutely, how people will relate to one another but can only place greater or lesser constraints upon the group members' capacity to organize how they will meet the task at hand.

The external system is a concept that invites us to look at how a group achieves what its members feel they must or need to do, if the group is to remain in that setting. For that reason the idea is most readily seen in settings where the environmental demands are themselves relatively clear. Homans chose a factory workshop as the example for introducing this concept, for there we can see how the relationships between the workers are constrained by the activities and the interactions which the company prescribed. In one sense it also provides us with a view of the group in its more formal aspect, a topic to which we will return later on in this chapter. With reference to the discussion in chapter 2 concerning what people feel they 'can do', the external system shows the pattern of activity in which certain actions and expressions are positively demanded and others are censured. For example, in the tutorial group it is expected that the people taking part will act as students and not as friends. This does not mean that they cannot be friendly, but that the matter at hand concerns the subject of study and not things which are part of their personal lives.

By making sentiment part of the environment, Homans makes it possible to think of it within the social sphere. The student who is always asking questions or who is keen to hand in a lengthy essay might be dismissed by some others as a 'creep' or a bore. However, this person can be seen as bringing to the group sentiments drawn from his or her membership of other groups to which he or she belongs. This makes possible a discussion of the ways in which characteristics associated with the membership of one group serve in the person's participation in a new or in another grouping. We shall take up this issue of multiple group membership as a central issue in the chapter to follow.

Finally, we should note that in bringing sentiments to a new group people bring more than abstract qualities. After all, these feelings are expressed through action, in particular ways. The male student who affects an air of 'I've seen it all before' or the female student who talks very quietly only in response to a direct question are bringing attitudes and expectations which derive from their peer groups and from their gender identities. While Homans does not elaborate upon the possibility, we can accept that one of the most important aspects of sentiment which people contribute as group members derives from their gender, and hence, their bodily condition. It is not just people or students who join the tutorial group, but, for example, 'five women and three men'. Whether this should or should not make a difference to how the tutorial proceeds is another matter, and one to which we shall return in the next chapter. In the meanwhile we need to examine the consequences of acting in terms of the demands of the environment. What happens when individuals meet in the tutorial, or ask each other for the loan of a book, or are required to work together in the first year practical class?

Developing group cohesion: the internal system

The simple consequence of having to deal with other group members is that people form likes and dislikes about each other. The organization of these sentiments, the activities that express them and the interactions which they sustain is called by Homans the *internal system*. Like its counterpart which has been described above, the internal system is a 'side' of group life and, together with the external system, provides a conceptual scheme for approaching the question of formality and informality in personal relationships. Taking the example of the new students who have arrived at college, the initial actions of the group are guided by what have been termed the demands of the setting, of the educational institution. As soon as they begin to deal with one another in the course of meeting these demands, they confront, reveal and recognize each other as different personalities. I have deliberately used the contrasting terms 'confront' and 'reveal' to indicate that, right from the beginning, people will address in different ways what they see as being the group's obligations. Homans proposes that, as a result of doing such things as asking a question in a tutorial, helping another student to find his way to the bookshop or co-operating with someone in the first-year practical class, there emerge sentiments of liking (or disliking) which then promote further interactions with those other people. For example, two students who go in search of the bookshop may discover that they have other things in common apart from finding themselves on the same degree course. As a result, they decide to go to the cinema together that day and to join the student drama society in which they have an interest. On the following day, they sit next to one another in the lecture and co-operate in getting books to prepare the first essay they will have to write. What is happening here is a microcosm of what is happening, in different ways (remember the dislikes too!), in the remainder of the class, so that after a few weeks an observer could see the beginnings of a pattern of relationships in the class as a whole.

The sentiments of liking and disliking, the activities which express these directly, and the interactions which can eventually be described as friendships and enmities constitute the internal system. Note that where I have chosen to introduce this in terms of two imaginary people, Homans explained it as happening in the group as a whole. Its effects can be seen when the class meets together, as pointed out above. The internal system refers, therefore, to feelings and activities in the group which refer, not to the demands of the environment, but to the informal relationships of the individuals concerned. It is most clearly observed in groups which are said to have a strong sense of identity or are seen to be cohesive, where the reasons for what the groups do are best sought in their members' feelings for one another, rather than in what they are obliged to do in their particular environments.

The relationship between the external and internal systems is important in Homans's analysis. First of all, they are the two essential components to group life; one cannot exist without the other. Second, the internal system is said to 'react back' upon the external, so as to alter it. As soon as group members form a liking (no matter how slight) for someone else, that sentiment will affect how they interact in the course of activities which are part of the external system. Homans gives the example of the worker who spends a little extra time handing over something to a workmate in order to spend a moment in conversation. We can easily imagine the help which one student might give another with a statistical problem because of such feelings. Equally, one can imagine the small group whose practical session fails to get going because two of the people involved do not like each other and resent the other's suggestions about how to proceed. In the larger group context, the reaction of the internal system upon the external is shown in the way that greater or lesser cohesion affects the way that the group's task will be done. However, one should not presume that the nature of this effect will inevitably be a foregone conclusion. In a study which examined the effect of group cohesion upon efficiency of problem solving, schoolchildren were organized into groups according to their preferences, some being arranged to be 'cohesive' and others to be 'less cohesive'. In the initial trials it was indeed found that the more cohesive groups were quicker at solving the problems set. However, as the experiment proceeded, this effect declined to the point where it all but vanished. The experimenters concluded that this was the result of the more cohesive groups spending time talking about what interested them rather than carrying out the task set. In this case the internal system served to hinder rather than to promote the group's goals in its particular setting and provides one instance of the possible relationship between these two complementary aspects of group life (Shaw and Shaw 1962).

From what has been said above it should be clear that all groups can be analysed in terms of both external- and internal-system relationships. Indeed, the strength of Homans's theory is that it enables us to discuss group life in terms of the relative balance and interdependence of these two features. Even at the beginning of a new group there will be the formation of first impressions which are the early flashes of internal-system sentiment. And no group can retire wholly into its own internal system without risking invalidating its relationship to the environment. If workers spend too much time in conversation, they risk being disciplined by the management; if students spend the practical class planning a holiday together rather than carrying out the exercise prescribed, they risk failing that course component.

Let me say a final word on external and internal systems as such. Nobody should expect to go and look at a group of people and expect to see either of these things, for 'things' they are not. These terms are *concepts* which form part of Homans's theory. Their value is in helping us to analyse what happens in different kinds of group, so that we can make sense of phenomena which would otherwise be difficult to talk about. And, of course, because of the reacting back of the internal upon the external system, even the simplest acts and interactions will display features of both.

The development of group structure: norms and 'sham' characteristics once again

The emergence of the internal system of relationships can be thought of as an *elaboration* of group activity; the students in our example do not just co-operate for the sake of doing the work but come to do so as part of extending their friendly relationship. Alongside this, and partly to facilitate it, group members tend towards a *standardization* of activity. This applies not only to what is done, but to how the group does it. In a factory the workers may adjust their output to a similar rate so that the pattern of their work is matched. This is less a matter of co-ordination than of activities becoming *entrained*, so that, for example, the pauses in their work patterns occur together and allow them to talk for a few moments (Moreland and Levine 1988). In any group, the larger issues in its life are helped by this standardization of the small happenings which, occurring regularly, are sometimes referred to as customs. These customary things can attain an importance quite beyond their usual proportion, such as when an outsider commits the error of doing things in a different way. When, over time, the group comes to have an awareness of the way it customarily does things, of the expected ways of behaviour of its members, we can talk of the group having *norms*. This is the term which social scientists use to summarize the pattern of expected ways of behaving in groups, being guidelines to the members as to what is expected of them and what might be allowed. Chapter 2 introduced the idea that expressive behaviour can be regarded as the making of a claim about oneself and about the kind of situation in which this happens. From the perspective of the group, it can be seen that the possibilities for claiming things about both of these things will be constrained by the norms to which individuals adhere.

Homans gave an example drawn from a study of men employed in the assembly of electrical components (the Bank Wiring Observation Room Study). The expectations which derived from the internal system had produced a situation in which the output of components was held down to a level which suited the culture of the group as a whole. Should any worker deviate too highly from this standard (producing either more or less), the other workers would informally chide him about this in order to bring him into line. In so doing they were making him aware of the norms concerning the group's output rate, a matter which was subject to informal as well as to formal (i.e. management) expectations of what was required. In this example, Homans also drew attention to the emergence of differential status within the group as a function of how individual members met the criteria attaching to group norms. Men with higher status tended to have a work output close to the standard set by the group. Being a leader, in these terms, means being the person who best embodies the norms of the group.

This can be illustrated by the way in which status and expectations work to constrain and thereby to control the behaviour of members of a street-corner gang, originally reported by W.F. Whyte in 1943 in his book *Street Corner Society* (1981) and used by Homans to develop his own theory of groups. Known as 'The Norton Street Gang', its members grew up in a poor area of the city populated by immigrant workers. The study took place during the depression of the 1930s, so that the reason for the group's existence lay in social and economic circumstances which provided its setting. The gang spent much of its time bowling, a form of relaxation which came to be an activity by which the group members could compare each other. Bowling and bowling standards were an important measure of a member's standing in the gang. The leader, Doc, was a good bowler, and his and other individuals' performances were known to the gang members. Among the weaker players was Alec, who was also one of the lower-status members of the team. On the occasion of one bowling match, Alec let it be known that he was going to do his best to win, and indeed after a while was leading by several pins. However, as the match progressed, the other players heckled him and he began to miss, eventually allowing his performance to collapse to last place in the team. After the match, Whyte (who had become a temporary gang member) asked Doc what would have happened if Alec had won. Doc's reply was that there would have been a lot of argument about the fact that this was a lucky event, not a true reflection of Alec's bowling ability. Another match would have to be arranged in order to put him in his place.

This is interesting because it shows, not that gang members bowled according to their status, but that where they threatened to bowl outside their 'proper position' the group exerted its influence to restore the *status quo*. Group norms do not work mechanically upon people but need to be expressed and (or) articulated through action and argument. In the case of the Norton Street Gang, these norms became the focus of argument because they were based upon something of significance to the group – bowling. Also, the norms which members share *with* each other *about* each other are there as enabling and hindering features of individual action. What Alec suffered in his fellow gang members' slights was an undermining of his claim to a higher status in the group; this he had hoped to achieve by raising his game to a higher level. The expectations which the others had of his ability were eventually confirmed through his own errors of play. This analysis brings us back to the argument concerning the circularity of 'sham', 'pseudo' and 'real' characteristics. In this case the sham qualities are those attributed to Alec as part of the group's (and his own) expectations of his behaviour, a confirmation of his low status. In the light of improvements in his real abilities (bowling score), and in his pseudo claims to higher status, these sham attributes were expressed forcibly to the point where his claim could no longer be substantiated in action.

The interdependence which we saw between the 'sham', 'pseudo' and 'real' characteristics is repeated in the circularity which Homans proposes between activity, sentiment and interaction, and more broadly between internal and external systems of relationship. What is commonly called confidence in the group setting is something which owes much to the expectations which members have about each other. This is why group members with low status can often find that they can do something alone, or with a particular friend, but somehow not be able to carry it off in the company of the group as a whole. This shows that claims which individuals have to be certain kinds of people are not wide open but are subject to the ways in which the norms of the group apply to them in particular. Leaders of groups have more scope than their followers to lay claim to be able to do various things, though even they are subject to the norms of the group. Paradoxically, Homans has argued that the group leader is *more* constrained by these norms, for, as the person who most closely embodies them, he or she must live up to those standards. In any event, we can see from this analysis that the development of relationships within the group depends upon the claims which people make effectively, as well as providing the basis from which both joint and individual claims will be maintained in future.

Taking the lead: some consequences of claiming expertise

So far in this chapter we have seen how social interaction can be understood in terms of group relationships which make up a system having both exernal and internal features. Remember that the former does not refer to relationships which the group has with people outside, but to its own ways of dealing with the demands of its environment. These may involve communicating with people outside, but it is the way in which the group does this as a group which makes the external system into what it is. Because these two facets of group action are interdependent, the members' individual actions and sentiments are inevitably a compound of these two features. Every time a student speaks in a tutorial, he or she does so within a system of relationships which is at once directed at furthering the group's educational task and in communicating a point of view. This will involve supporting, or undermining, the points made by others in the group. We are all caught, to a greater or to a lesser degree, in expressing sentiments of a personal and an impersonal kind, through actions which are guided by expectations that we are both members of the group (e.g. the tutorial) and individual persons, (our 'selves'). In this section I want to pursue the question of how these two aspects of social interaction emerge and interrelate in the course of group life.

The work which relates closely to this issue was carried out some years ago by Robert F. Bales (1950, 1958). Sometimes this work is reported in the context of the methodology which he devised for recording group communication (Interaction Process Analysis), but more often it is cited as having given rise to a particular theory of leadership in small groups. Neither of these aspects is of major concern for us here, because the focus of interest is the two forms of communication which Bales recorded, and the implications of these for our discussion of ambiguity in social life. Broadly speaking, Bales put forward a view not unlike that of Homans, in which group communication has two main faces, a *task-oriented* one and what he termed a *social-emotional* one. His theory was also based upon the idea of the group as a system, in which stability was maintained through the changing balance of these two forms of communication. Task orientation is a term intended to summarize verbal (or non-verbal) exchanges which bear either directly or indirectly upon the task at hand.

In his experiment, Bales used groups of five men who were given a real-life problem to solve. Because the men did not know each other beforehand, they also had the problem of getting themselves organized to achieve the task which had been set them. It was in the course of expressing their feelings towards each other that the group members also communicated in ways which had a social or emotional content. The studies of Bales and his colleagues involved the experimenters in detailed coding of everything that the group members said and did during the course of the problem-solving discussions. The same groups were asked to take part in several such sessions, allowing the men to establish relationships with each other over the course of their meetings. During the investigation, the group members were asked to say which of their fellows they liked or disliked, and who they thought had produced the best ideas. It was discovered that the member in each group who was felt by his colleagues to have had the best ideas was indeed the person who had initiated many of the attempts at solving the problem, making suggestions and giving opinions on other people's ideas. In comparison, the best-liked men were more likely to have said things which increased the feeling of common ground among the members; where necessary they made jokes or defused potential arguments. On the basis of these results, Bales put forward the hypothesis that groups organize themselves through a process of *role differentiation*, in which there emerges a member who is a *task specialist* and one who is a *social-emotional specialist*. This is the hypothesis that groups operate under the leadership of two different kind of leaders (the *dual-status hypothesis*), one focusing upon the task at hand and one upon 'oiling the wheels', so to speak, of the relationships between the members.

It has been said that both Bales's theory and that of Homans share a view of the group as a system of relationships. In a more immediate way the two theories also focus upon the same kind of duality in group life, in which relationships concern either the task or the personal concerns of the members. More formally we can compare them as follows:

HOMANS		BALES
External system	is to	Task orientation
	as	
Internal system	is to	Social-emotional orientation

Making this comparison should not be taken as an assertion that these two theorists mean the same things by their respective concepts. The purpose of putting them alongside each other in this way is to highlight the fact that they are dealing with similar issues in the way people act together in groups. For both Bales and Homans argue that the development of relationships proceeds through a process of role differentiation, in which individuals come to play particular parts in the life of the group. This involves a specialization of their contributions and, according to Bales's hypothesis, a complementarity of leadership roles. Role differentiation depends, however, on there being some consensus among the members as to what the group as a whole is trying to achieve.

Before we review Bales's findings regarding the effect of consensus on role differentiation, it is worth reminding ourselves of the relevance of this work for our earlier concern with the work of appearances in social interaction. When we were discussing expressive behaviour, it was argued that the characters which people established for themselves depended upon there being some agreement or consensus as to the validity of the performances which individuals put forward. If a group of ramblers lose their way in the countryside, and one of their number assumes an attitude of confident leadership, will his (or her) claim to be a knowledgeable and reliable guide be accepted by the others? And does another individual's reassuring and conciliatory remarks establish his (or her) claim to be the person to co-ordinate the feelings of the group?

Bales (1958) found that the emergence of the two different kinds of leader was facilitated by high initial consensus among group members. (This was defined as the agreement among the rankings made by group members of each other.) In these groups one person established himself as a task specialist, while another was the social specialist in the discussions. Early on in the research it had been shown that the former role (the 'ideas man') was associated with being less well liked as the meetings progressed. Being the most liked person was the main attribute of the social specialist. The question therefore arose, why is the person acknowledged to have the best ideas for solving the problem not the most well-liked individual? It would seem that whether or not people see themselves as equals in the group makes an important difference (one to which we will return shortly). Where people do see themselves as having the same initial status in the group, making effective contributions to solving the task at hand is to gain prestige at the risk of being resented. Others in the group may wonder, 'Who is s/he to keep talking, and telling the rest of us what to do?' Bales and his colleagues found that the ideas men were people prepared to face a certain amount of negative feeling and were also prepared to be critical of others and to show whom they did and did not like. In contrast, the people in each group whom the others liked best (the social specialist) tended to like the others to an equal degree.

It would appear that the dynamics of the situation were as follows. The person who suggested what to do was recognized for his ability but nonetheless resented for his presumption, and perhaps for his way of showing disregard for the suggestions of others. As a consequence, discontent and bad feeling were aroused towards him which was expressed indirectly through the positive feelings shown to another member who was seen to be a worthy recipient. This latter person, the social specialist, was described by Bales (1958) as a 'symbolic transmuter of negative affect' in the group. This means that the group members were able to convert the discontent which the task specialist aroused into positive feeling, by focusing upon their relationships rather than upon the task exclusively. The group could then continue to run under the rubric of this 'dual-status leadership', which formed an inner wheel of communication within the wider sphere of interaction.

For the purposes of this discussion, what is interesting about this occurrence is that it is not an inevitable or mechanical process, in spite of being described as the workings of a 'system of relationships'. By putting forward a suggestion, or by criticizing someone else's proposal, the ideas man makes a claim to be able to direct the group which, if it is to be substantiated, requires that this line of action be followed up. In Goffman's terms, it is not only the suggestion given which matters, but also the information given off. In this case, the information given off concerns the claim to be, perhaps, knowledgeable about the problem, to be insightful and to be decisive in one's judgement. The ideas man in Bales's groups can substantiate this claim only by being consistent, and this involves dropping claims (if he ever made them) to being concerned primarily with the effect of his remarks upon other people's sensibilities. Once the efficacy of his suggestions is demonstrated, and once the others acknowledge his claim to speak for the group on the matter of the problem at hand, then the specialization of roles has occurred, and in future meetings he will not have to press his claim alone. Then, the expectations of the other group members will facilitate his position, not only in their deference to his authority on formal matters of the task, but by their frequent direction of informal remarks towards the social-emotional specialist.

As mentioned above, Bales's work is often presented as the discovery that there are 'two kinds of leaders' in a group. In fact, Bales also recognized that the task and the social-emotional roles can, on occasions, be played by a single person, and that in some groups this role differentiation occurs in only a sporadic and tentative manner. These two kinds of communication are not entirely separate things but are both expressed, to a greater or a lesser degree, by *all* group members. Just as Homans's analysis showed that group interaction involves both external- and internal-system relationships, so the differentiation of roles emerges out of individual contributions stemming from both task and social concerns. The picture which is sometimes drawn, of groups' consisting of an unfriendly person who produces only good ideas, a popular individual who makes only encouraging and supportive remarks, and a neutral following, is but a shallow account of Bales's contribution to this field. Task leaders were not wholly disliked but were found to be liked less than some other members; social specialists did not only make friendly remarks, but also contributed to the task function in their communications to the task leader. In general, the consequence of role specialization is that each individual in the group enlarges his or her scope of action in some areas and limits that scope in other spheres. This occurs as part of a system of relationships in which these varied claims are more or less known to all group members.

Legitimacy and the paradox of authority

The differentiation of roles in the groups which Bales studied was conditional upon there being some *consensus* among the group members about what they were about, some common culture of basic premises. In groups where consensus among members remained low, any differentiation of roles observed was said to have been there from the beginning, rather than to have emerged in the course of the discussion. The participants appeared to act on the basis of their previous personalities, rather than in terms of a group structure to which they jointly contributed. Any group which is to develop requires of its members that they both become more similar in certain ways (Homans's 'standardization') and different in other ways ('differentiation'). Achieving these consistencies and discontinuities is not always easy, for it requires each person to give up something of his or her own, and to take on something of other people's. The situation of low consensus reflects a paradox which is well known in groups which meet for psychotherapy. Here participants sometimes act in ways which preserve both the group and their own individuality at the same time. It has been claimed that groups which fail to achieve a definite culture are the result of their members' clinging to a common, but unarticulated, standpoint. Within this each member can at one time hide his or her individuality (thus preventing it from being challenged) and collectively resist the group's development. The latter aim derives from the need to avoid the debates and the demands which inevitably flow from people trying to encourage the group to 'get somewhere', or to solve a problem.

This kind of group is not restricted to the clinic, because the problem does not lie in the 'pathology' of psychotherapy patients. The apparent threat of the group's authority and of the loss of our individuality is common to everyone who participates in social life. Take, for example, the seminar group. It is not unusual to find that a group of students who have prepared adequately for the meeting will sit silently until the tutor speaks, only replying when asked a question. For those readers who have never been tutors, I can tell you that taking such a seminar can be hard going. Oddly enough, when one individual makes a point, the other students do not pick it up and elaborate it, but leave it to wither, quietly, at our feet. If someone begins to say a great deal, this seems only to make matters worse, as the other students become even more committed to a policy of non-participation, to the point of showing signs of irritation with the speaker. From the point of view of the tutor, the students seem, individually, interested only in making points to him, yet collectively concerned to hinder each other's particular contributions. While it might be true to say that the group has a low consensus about which of them might lead the discussion, they enjoy a high consensus as to the danger to the group of any such discussion's starting at all. For if it does, then each of them, as individuals, will be required to make his or her contribution in ways which will demand achieving a common ground and establishing different points of view. The unspoken consensus is that it will be less hazardous to each individual student if they do not engage in intellectual debate in which some claims will (perhaps) be supported, and some claims (almost certainly) will be challenged and exposed as false.

This example, based freely upon the work of the British psychotherapist W.I. Bion (1961), is not intended as a critique of tutorial groups, still less of students. (Reading Bion's work will show that the group leader (tutor) has a key role in the development of group culture.) It shows that the idea that relationships are based upon the consensual validation of what each of us claims to be requires some qualification. The notion that social life involves people playing discrete roles suggests that we have no choice in the matter, and that group life can only accentuate the differences between us. This example shows that it is possible for people to use groups as ways of obscuring that individuality, of hindering the requirement that each person stake a claim to be a particular kind of individual. It may be that this is more likely to occur when people feel threatened, such as when they meet in psychotherapy groups or with fellow students of uncertain critical power and temperament. It certainly seems to happen in some situations where the participants are of equal status in that group, so that who has the right to speak on the issue is a matter to be determined in open debate, when claim and counter-claim must be actively enjoined.

Support for this suggestion comes from another quarter, where critics have considered the limitations of Bales's findings for groups in various sections of society. One of the main issues is that of the legitimacy of the leader, or to put it more simply, whether the group members accept the right of the leader to occupy that role (Burke 1973). Remember that the diverting of positive feeling toward the social specialist was dependent upon the resentment of the claims of the ideas man. This implies that role differentiation in the group happens because of this resentment, because of the other group members' feeling of 'Why him and not me, or that pleasant chap over there?' In groups where the person making the suggestions is accepted from the beginning as the leader, then resentment would be inappropriate and, indeed, the emergence of a dual-status order would not be expected to occur. In the company boardroom, the chairman (rarely, chairwoman) does not have to claim the right to direct how the board should proceed, nor is he resented by his colleagues for chairing the meeting; he is expected to do so. Although there have been many applications of Bales's methodology to group situations of different kinds, his results would appear to reflect something of the nature of the groups which he studied, abstracted from the institutions of society. This does not mean, however, that this work is of less value than first claimed. Arguably it teaches us a further lesson, that the scope for making and for sustaining relationships is constrained by the social order. This should not surprise us, given that we began this discussion of relationships acknowledging that 'pseudo' and 'sham' characteristics depended upon social differences for their power to discriminate between and to form evaluations of other people.

Finally in this section, we should note that the paradox of authority and independence will tend to re-emerge when the accepted and legitimated leader of the group is under threat or attack. In the Norton Street Gang we saw how, in the free competition of a bowling match, members 'chivvied' one individual who threatened to overturn the accepted status hierarchy of the group. In Bion's accounts of his psychotherapy groups, there is a similar description of how one patient who tried to usurp the role of the leader (doctor) was undermined by the remainder of the patients. Once acknowledged as the 'leader' or the spokesperson, or more particularly as the doctor or the tutor, this individual has certain rights and obligations which are embodied in the workings of the group, not just in his or her own thoughts and feelings.

Formality and informality: the group experience

In the two analyses which have been made in this chapter, both Homans's and Bales's theories have shown that group life is made up of activities related to the task at hand, and those which are related to the personal relationships of the members. In the one case, we saw that the group's ethos was a product of these two systems' working together, the external and the internal. In the case of Bales's theory, every member was seen to be involved in making contributions to the problem with which the group was faced, and to the socio-emotional concerns of fellow members. If one looks at groups where the balance of these two aspects is very one-sided, one way or the other, one can identify certain groups as being mainly concerned with doing the job at hand (guided by external-system requirements) and other groups which seem to live only for themselves, so to speak (operating under the guidance of the internal system). Good examples of the first kind include work groups, committees and military groups of all types, The crew of a battleship going into action exemplifies the system of relationships in which action, sentiment and interaction are committed with respect to the demands of the environment. These demands include all aspects of fighting to stay alive and to destroy the enemy. By comparison, groups which operate mainly in terms of the internal system include friendship groups where the demands of the environment are either limited or diminished for one reason or another. We might want to hold on to this distinction in order to compare 'formal groups' with 'informal groups' in order to say how relationships are different in each case. One of the problems with doing this is that it is unlikely to lead to more than a detailing of the main distinction already drawn. A more fundamental problem is that, to stay with this simple classification, we should need to divide all the 'grey areas' in our analysis into 'black' or 'white'. Unfortunately we should soon find that we do not have formal *or* informal groups, if by this we mean something like military bands versus coffee parties. Instead, we would be faced with groups whose relationships to their environments are more or less well defined, and of a greater or a lesser complexity. The actual relationships of the people in groups always tend to be a complex of the external and the internal, the task and the socio-emotional.

It is common sense to know that people's relationships alter as the group setting changes. Sailors who have operated under strict rules of conduct while at sea may attempt to joke with their superiors as they leave the ship for a spot of leave. A group of student friends may find their relationships strained by a lecturer who makes them compete for grades on a course, or even by the onset of examinations and the prospect of variable results. Yet apart from these examples, the ideas which have been examined in this chapter suggest that the essence of group life is the ever present mix of the formal and the informal. Where we, as students of social interaction, try to separate them from each other, we diminish the problem rather than illuminate it. Take, for example, the attempt to apply Bales's ideas to the nuclear family. The separation of task and socio-emotional functions has been suggested to align with the division of labour between the sexes, so that husbands are responsible for the instrumental jobs (bringing in the money, digging the garden, etc.) while wives carry out all the caring functions (loving the different family members in spite of their various shortcomings, tending Johnny's knee when he falls over, etc.). We should not be too ready to scoff at this caricature because, although it has been shown not to reflect the actual state of affairs, it does tell us something about how the institution of marriage is still regarded by many people today.

In one experiment (Leik 1963), fathers, mothers and daughters were brought together (a) as whole families, (b) as representatives from different families (one father, one mother, one daughter), and (c) as groups of same role members (i.e. all fathers, all mother, all daughters). Using a Bales-type coding scheme, it was found that, although the fathers showed more task behaviour when placed together, and with a stranger wife and daughter, they were not more instrumental in their behaviour than the rest of their own family when all were together. Mothers tended to adopt a dual role, sharing the task sphere with their husbands and the emotional sphere with their daughters. Most important from our point of view is that this shows that the kind of behaviour in which people engage in groups is a function of the group's *visibility* to other groups. It would seem that, though the husbands might have been just as emotional as their wives in the privacy of their own homes, when in public the men felt that they must live up to the image of what a 'proper husband' should be like. If we extend this finding to other areas of life, it suggests that the balance of formality and informality which we might see in group relationships depends upon the members' awareness of their openness to scrutiny by other people. It confirms that one of the important features of the external system is the expectations which other groupings (or society in general) have for the group in question, or for particular people in the group. 'Smartening up', 'putting on a good show', 'looking one's best', are all terms which evoke the idea of the group shifting the basis of its action towards the external system.

I want to return to the issue of what is overlooked by separating out the formal from the informal in social life, for each of these can sometimes appear to emerge out of the other. For example, few environments can be as demanding as the battlefield, when relationships are governed by military rules of conduct. Paradoxically, it would seem that under these conditions strong friendships can be formed, when the scope for the expression of informality in the group is strictly limited. Indeed, it is under conditions of extreme danger, when the task of group survival is imperative, that sentiments of affection or of hatred are sometimes forged. It might be that the very limitation of the scope for friendship makes its appearance so much more highly valued. Certainly its endorsement in acts which reflect this 'reacting back' of the internal upon the external system is recognized in the awarding of medals and honours to the individuals concerned ('action over and above the call of duty').

These critical comments can also be made about groups which would appear to exist only as friendship groups, with little or no formal demands from the environment. Gangs, for example, might appear to fall into this category, and yet they are made up of individuals who are part of society by virtue of their gender, race or creed, to take some key characteristics. The Norton Street Gang is reported to have frozen out a member who made it clear that he intended to marry a girl whose moral standing the rest of the gang thought could jeopardize their own position. During the years of the Nazi party's rise to popular power, many ordinary Germans and Austrians had to choose what to do about someone who was a good friend and part of the group, but a Jew. One can only imagine the hand-wringing and justifications which some groups engaged in when discussing where their wider duty lay, as opposed to the sentiments of affection which the members could no longer afford to entertain.

A less emotive and more everyday example is to be found in the problems faced by students who decide to share a house or flat off campus. Having met at college and found that they have got on well in classes and outside, what could be more obvious than to share a house together? Many students have done this successfully. Others find that it does not work out, for the simple reason that the person whom you thought you knew is not the same person when it comes to doing a proper share of the shopping, washing up or contributing to the telephone bill. Analysing this example, we can say that a group operating explicitly under the internal system (friendship) precipitates a new environment which makes its own demands upon the group. In this case, rather than the internal system's seeming to emerge out of the external, the relationship is reversed. Now a group which believes it runs along lines of friendship finds that the relationships between members must be structured according to demands of their setting which, if not met or resolved, will lead to the decline or possible break-up of the group. Its members must now work out these demands within the friendship culture which they have established. Having to solve formal tasks within informal relationships may or may not make this easier to achieve. One way of sorting things out is to try to devise a system (external) for getting the jobs done, although it can be seen that, though this helps, it does not remove the necessity for the students to support this arrangement *because* they are friends.

Legitimation and the scope for appearances

From what we have seen so far it is clear that we can make few generalizations about groups and appearances. Different groups, with different relationships to their environmental settings, and with different internal cultures, will clearly vary in the ways in which members express themselves. Perhaps the most helpful idea that we have met in this chapter is that of *legitimation*, when the group members accept that a certain person will occupy a particular role in the group. The effect of this is to credit that person with the rights, and indeed the duty, to act in ways expected of someone in that position. In the Norton Street Gang, Doc was the leader and expected to act as such by the gang members. This did not mean that he could do anything he liked, but it meant that his scope for action was broader than that of other gang members. When lower-status members made suggestions, these did not carry the same weight as Doc's ideas, nor did their claim to speak for the group in that respect appear as valid. Anyone who has been in a group from its beginning knows that with the emergence of another individual as leader, the scope of one's own personal claims is diminished in certain respects. In other ways, however, they may be enhanced through one's membership of the group as a whole. A person who fails to be elected captain of the college hockey team might nevertheless benefit from the successes of the team and from its enhanced reputation. Even though such individuals might lack the 'pseudo' qualities which accrue to being captain, they might yet have their ('real') abilities enhanced by the 'sham' qualities surrounding the team's public image.

It is not only the position of individuals in the group which become legitimized, but also the norms and culture of the group itself. When a group is busy solving a problem under the guidance of its task leader, the ethos of the group is one of work. In this situation the expected mode of operation is one of relative seriousness, of getting on with the job at hand. Even in so-called informal groups, there are times for serious action, for serious talking. Then the joker, the dissenter and the uncommitted need to watch out, for the claims which they implicitly make in the pun, the sarcastic laugh or the barely stifled yawn are liable to be met with sanction. This means actions or words which carry the message, 'What you say is not worth saying, and your status in the group is in question.' Such breaches of group ethos, of marring the appearance which the group is fashioning for itself, need not be deliberate or things of which people are conscious. In his descriptions of a psychotherapy group, Bion (1961) makes special mention of the resentment provoked by a man and a woman who enter a meeting, late, in each other's company, and laughing together. Bion's interpretation of what follows is that the group regards the pair's behaviour as in some sense insulting to the group's claim to be working in the way that it is, and to express a relationship between the two which suggests an undue and base interest in each other. In the eyes of the group, and from the position it is trying to establish, the couple's departure from the behaviour expected is to be discredited, particularly by implying something which might not be the case, i.e. their sexual interest in each other. Only by seeing that the group makes some appearances legitimate but not others, can we understand how and why the claims made by some individuals are welcomed, though they seem outrageous, while others are undermined, though they seem to an outsider to be innocuous.

4

SOCIAL IDENTITY: THE CROSSROADS OF GROUP INVOLVEMENTS

In the previous chapter I tried to show that interaction is worked out in groups which have differing relationships to their environments. One consequence of this is variation in the way that people's roles in groups become differentiated. Terms such as 'task' and 'socio-emotional leader' reflect the fact that any group needs to be understood in terms of features which arise from environmental demands. One aspect of the external system mentioned in that context was the sentiment which individuals bring from other groups to which they belong. It is not just the physical and technical aspects of the environment which exert their demands upon the group, but also those aspects which people carry with them. These are things which may be hidden from view (remember the earlier discussion of 'visibility' in relationships), but often cannot be so. The more obvious examples are gender, age and physical condition. Less obvious are things like physical handicaps, such as having a glass eye, and characteristics such as accent and tone of voice. Because we carry them with us, these characteristics are there, to a greater or lesser degree, for others to see and to use as the basis for judging us.

In some situations these things are relevant to the definition of the group. For example, to be a member of Alcoholics Anonymous one should be physically dependent upon alcohol; outsiders, social drinkers and teetotallers are not normally welcome at AA group meetings. In contrast to these examples, there are groups where one's physical status, religious and ethnic background are deemed to be irrelevant, so that there are laws in the UK, as in other countries, concerning the abuse of such differences in the appointment of employees. One of the reasons why we need such laws is precisely because these features are used as indices of social differences, about which people often hold strong views, if not prejudices. For members of minority groups in particular, the issue of who they are (their *social identity*) is tied up with the scope of action which they can claim as members of *multiple groupings* in society. In this chapter we shall explore the relationship between these two aspects of social life, with the twin aims of extending our knowledge of group dynamics and of clarifying what we mean when speaking of the 'self' in social interaction.

Groups, cliques and the problem of emergence

In his description of the study carried out in a factory making electrical products, Homans describes how the men in the Bank Wiring Observation Room had divided into two cliques. Each of these cliques developed its own style of working, level of output and informal activities. The cliques were, in each of these respects, distinct. The group at the front of the room (clique A) worked on a slightly more complex task than the group at the back (clique B). The members of clique A felt that their activities were superior to those of clique B, and this extended to their informal games and conversation. The latter sub-group discussed less and indulged in more noise and horseplay than the former. The implied superiority of the men in clique A was resented by their fellows in clique B, who expressed this in ways which they knew would irritate the other men; they bickered and played around noisily. In response, the members of clique A heckled them for their low work output and time wasting which, though it had the desired effect of keeping them in their place, was said to strengthen the internal solidarity of the subordinate group still further.

This example raises a number of questions for us to address. It suggests that groups are not always unitary, but consist of sub-groupings which relate to one another as well as acting as cliques in their dealings with people outside. How do these cliques arise, and along what lines do they form? A further question arises from the observation made by Homans that the dominant clique A adhered more closely than did the other to the norms of the group as a whole. Given this to be the case, the question arises as to how certain cliques or individuals come to identify themselves more closely with the aims of the group as a whole. Is this purely a result of the interactions which have taken place in the course of the group's life, or are there other reasons why some people have a larger say in the direction which the group as a whole will take?

One answer to the question of how cliques form in groups is implicit in the account given by Homans. He noted that it was the technical level of the men's work which, at least superficially, provided the basis for their distinguishing themselves. Men who carried out the more precise jobs worked next to each other and therefore talked together. In the case of groups which meet outside the work situation, the distinctions which are made upon us through the division of labour (the secretary, the miner) still operate. We know them best in terms of social class and gender, to which social types we allocate each other on first meeting. These features are known as *external-status characteristics*, and their place in the dynamics of group meetings has received attention in social psychological research.

The effect of external-status characteristics upon a group was examined in a study involving people who had been called for jury duty (Strodtbeck, James and Hawkins 1957). They were asked to listen to a recorded trial, to deliberate on the evidence and then come up with a verdict. The jurors formed a cross-section of the population of Chicago and St Louis, being made up of men and women from different walks of life – business people, clerical, skilled and unskilled workers. Their discussions were recorded and transcribed, allowing an analysis to be made of the contributions of each member. It was found that men talked more than women, as did business and clerical people more than skilled and unskilled workers. The jurors had been asked to elect a foreman at the outset. Comparing across the different occupational groups, it was found that in the case of business people they were elected more often than expected, while unskilled workers, in particular, were chosen far less often than expected. (Expectation here refers to the assumption that members of the groups would be elected in proportion to their makeup of the jury groups.)

These results suggest that people's social class will influence how they see their potential contribution to the group ('Should I speak up or leave it to them?'), and how others think class affects organizing ability. At the beginning of the discussions the jurors were asked, individually, to state their verdict, and then this was compared with the subsequent group decision. There was a close relationship between what business people had decided individually and the eventual jury decision which was not found for the other occupational groupings. Also, when asked to choose what kind of person they would like to hear a case brought against a member of their own family, jurors of every background chose business people above all others. The social class of those involved appears to have determined not only how they contributed, but how those contributions were perceived by their fellow jurors.

One immediate question concerns the lasting effect of these status differences. Do they affect the members of the group throughout its workings and discussion? Reference to the jury study suggests that this is not so. When asked later in the meeting which of their fellow jurors they would choose to hear a case in which they themselves were on trial, the tendency to choose higher-status persons had declined. The effect of the face-to-face discussions was to allow the individuals to base their choices upon experience, rather than upon stereotypes and views of their own interest groups. This finding should not surprise us, although we should be prepared to take on the implications of what this means for explaining how people act in groups. First of all, any interpretation of this study in terms of people's contributions being 'determined' by their class membership must be inadequate. The fact that this was overcome, if but partially in some cases, shows that we are dealing here with assumptions which people make, and upon which they act. We may call them perceptions or stereotypes but not 'causes', which suggests a mindlessness which goes against all experience of social life. Enough has already been said in this book to indicate that social class in the group context is something assumed by actor and observer in their turn; it bears something of both 'pseudo' and 'sham' qualities in its expressive and impressive features. This means that people can either adopt a class category and accentuate their claim to embody it, or they can act in ways that are difficult to pin down as being, for example, either middle or working class.

What makes the jury study interesting is its relevance to what we know about differences in society, particularly the inequality of opportunity and distribution of power. It suggests that, far from the norms of groups being developed by all members equally, some individuals have a larger hand in establishing what the group ought to be doing and what its priorities should be. Just as the Bank Wiring Observation Room study revealed two cliques of unequal status, based upon a distinction in work complexity, so the jury study points up the possibility of unequal sub-groups based upon external-status characteristics. Later on we shall discuss the conditions under which status characteristics are either retained or transformed in the course of developing new relationships within the group. For the moment we need to say more about inequalities, for this issue raises questions of identity as well as those of group structure.

Inequalities in group membership

To be a member of the subordinate clique in a group is to taste both sweet and bitter fruits, often at the same time. While social psychologists have not examined the problem in these terms, they have shown how people who feel themselves less highly valued in terms of a central criterion adopt other criteria on which they can make a better showing. In the Bank Wiring Observation Room study, members of clique B believed that they had more fun at work than those in clique A, who more nearly met the norms of the group as a whole. Although State Registered Nurses have been recognized as being of higher status by their less qualified State Enrolled Nurse colleagues in terms of specific abilities, the latter were shown to see themselves as superior when it came to matters of co-operation vital for providing emotional care (Skevington 1981). Nevertheless, members of subordinate groups remain so because the group as a whole is defined by the qualities which are held by the dominant sub-grouping. The bitter-sweetness to which I referred above arises when subordinate groups act in ways which simultaneously express their own identity (in contrast to the dominant grouping) and thereby confirm their position in the group as secondary. When clique B broke out into noisy horseplay or swopped jobs between themselves in ways not approved of by management, they did this to affirm their own group identity and to irritate members of clique A. However, in terms of the need for the group to meet certain output goals, and to show skill in the execution of their tasks, clique B revealed themselves to fall short of the group expectations.

Social psychologists have examined how people in groups of different status make judgements about one another. In particular, studies have been carried out which have examined the effect of varying the numerical balance of the majority/minority and the value judgement (status) placed upon each grouping. These experiments involved assessing the amount of favouritism that members would extend to members of their own group when asked to carry out an allocation of some reward determined by the investigator. For example, in one study it was found that among students at a Welsh university, the Welsh showed more in-group favouritism than the English (Branthwaite and Jones 1975). Given the political and economic differences in favour of the English, this finding supports a view of the subordinate group as being relatively solidary in the face of the group holding higher status. However, this need not necessarily be the case.

We can easily imagine the conditions under which this situation might change, and consider the perception of events from both sides of the boundary. The aspects which vary are the relative status of the cliques and the extent of the imbalance in the majority/minority of all concerned. In a study designed to examine these conditions, individuals were divided into groups on the basis of a test which they were told was a measure of creativity. They were then asked to distribute a series of rewards either to members of their own group, or to those of another which was different in terms of the supposed creativity measure. The aim of the study was to discover which particular mix of status and numerical balance would produce the greatest effect of in-group favouritism, a measure of the solidarity of the clique so created (Moscovici and Paichelier 1978).

Results showed that high in-group favouritism was shown by members of two particular groupings. Those who believed themselves to be of higher status and in the minority were interpreted as needing to bolster their position against the 'threat' of the lower-status majority. These latter subjects, who believed themselves to be of lower status and in the majority, also showed in-group favouritism, possibly because they were in a position to rival the favoured minority. Moderate levels of in-group favouritism were shown by low-status subjects who were in the minority, some clearly accepting the dominance of the high-status majority. It is in this condition, where members are both in a numerical minority and where their ideas and activities are denigrated or undermined, that there is the greatest reason for them to accept the 'natural superiority' of the dominant grouping. The lowest levels of in-group favouritism were shown by the group which believed itself to be of high status and in the majority. In this case, their generosity to the minority, lower-status group can be interpreted more generally as a kind of condescension. This occurs where a group is so confident of its position that it can afford, without risk to itself, to make gestures to members of the subordinate group. This combination of status difference and a clear imbalance in group membership is strengthened where there is a stability in this inequality, so that people in the dominant group feel secure in the 'rightness' of the world, while people in the subordinate group accept the *status quo* without seeing the possibility of changing the situation.

One example of this last-mentioned situation is to be found in the entry of women into spheres of work traditionally regarded as a male preserve. The recruitment of a woman into a male-dominated setting creates a situation in which there is a gross imbalance between the sexes, and in which the woman can appear as a token of her gender. In a study of the sales departments of American firms which employed just one or two women, it was found that the women were more visible, in that they captured more of the group's awareness (Kanter 1977). This heightened visibility meant that their technical abilities were clouded by their physical appearance. As a consequence, the women had to work harder to make their technical abilities more apparent, but in doing this they risked being labelled as aggressive by their male colleagues. This ambivalence is a further example of how efforts by minority members to be distinct are seen as undermining, while their efforts to comply with the majority risk being seen as pushiness. On the part of the men, this ambivalence was accentuated by their acceptance of the woman into the group on the understanding that she accept their traditional (male) values and actions. If she did not, then her difference 'as a woman' was pointed out to her; if she did accept, she colluded in what amounted to a denigration of other members of her sex.

We can see here that being a member of a lower-status group in the world of the majority places particular, and sometimes quite complicated, constraints upon how one can act in face-to-face relationships. In the case of the women described above, this meant treading a line between asserting one's rights and satisfying the demands of the work environment. If we take this back to the language of appearances, their situation was one of trying to make a claim to be an efficient and a reliable worker in a context in which their actions were also being read as gender signs by their male colleagues. This ambivalence cannot be overcome by the minority group member alone, because the expectations about how they should act, about the identities which they bear, are collectively held by the people with whom they come into contact. This ambiguity of expectation is not restricted to social types such as gender and racial groups. The handicapped and the disfigured are also prey to the expectations of the physically complete and the healthy. Goffman (1963) has noted that we expect these people to act as if they were 'normal', but they must not act 'normally'. So, for example, a facially disfigured person should act naturally in our presence so as not to cause embarrassment, but he or she should not presume to kiss us.

Clearly the claims which people may make to be certain kinds of individuals, and the part which they might play in groups which they join are subject to the social valuation placed upon other groups to which they are deemed to belong. Certain statuses which individuals enjoy or suffer are, to differing degrees, borne openly by them (e.g. skin colour, gender) and must therefore be both the basis and often the subject of group attention. They are the basis of group relationships in embodying the expectations ('sham' qualities) which people have of each other at the outset, empowering some to speak up and committing others to silence or to having their opinions not taken seriously. They are the subject of group attention at points where they might be exploited for the group's aims ('Go on, you girls, do the washing up'), or where a member of a lower-status group transgresses the expectations set for that group and claims the rights normally assumed by the dominant clique.

As a final point, it should be noted that the particular balance or imbalance of cliques in groups, or of representation of different social types, is not in itself a determinant of how individuals relate to one another. It is better to think of these as limitations to which people accede and which they yet attempt to overcome. The social and the psychological bases of action which make this possible will be the focus of attention in the later parts of this chapter. First, let us review some of the arguments put forward earlier in the book in the light of the points made in this chapter so far.

Some assumptions about appearances and groups reviewed

In the course of the last half-dozen pages the reader may have been struck by an unintended ambiguity concerning the word 'group'. Some of the time the word has been used to apply to the whole set of people under consideration, while at other times I have used it to indicate what is, in fact, a sub-grouping or clique. The ambiguity arises because both of these phenomena exist at the same time. Around the table at Christmas is the whole family in splendid unity, but the children are denied the alcohol offered to all the adults, and so go off to the kitchen to get more lemonade. If the family is large enough, then different branches of it will have distinct interests about what did or did not happen in the past, and what should happen in the future (particularly about who should inherit which items). However, even in their division over something, the different branches may come together in the face of criticism of the family name by someone from outside ('blood is thicker than water'). All this might happen in the space of a single mealtime, so that 'James', at 12 years of age, might experience himself first as a child (rather than an adult), then as a member of the whole family, then as a 'Smith' rather than a 'Jones', and finally as part of the whole family once again.

In each of these brief episodes, an observer would need to draw and to redraw the boundaries of what are to be considered the groups in question. The idea that the group *is* the family is only tenable if we also credit the sub-groupings with their own identity as units of some kind. In social psychological research which has traditionally investigated relationships in the laboratory, this issue has often not arisen because the isolation of the subjects and their abstraction from the real settings in which they live have guaranteed that the experimenter could say unequivocably that the six people sitting round the table were 'the group'. (This was true for the groups which Bales studied.) The attention to the relationship between cliques and the group as a whole, such as was provided by Homans in his analysis, is a much rarer event, and provides an additional reason for including his ideas in this book. More usual in social psychological studies of cliques is that they are treated as if they were two quite separate groupings, the experimenter paying little or no attention to the whole group. This was true even in the classic study reported by Sherif (1966) in which two groups of boys at summer camp were separated and allowed to develop distinct identities. As a result members of each faction increased their in-group solidarity during competitive activities and showed aggression and tension towards those in the competing group. This work set a trend for the study of what psychologists call intergroup-relations research. The fact that the boys comprised a wider group in relation to the camp and the experimenters is generally overlooked. It is this relationship between a group and its environment to which Homans drew attention, for it provides the basis for the two factions being there at all.

This criticism is more important than perhaps it first appears. It suggests that, where social psychologists have looked either at a single, self-contained group of people in the laboratory, or else at the relationship between two distinct sub-groupings, they have been missing out the crucial relationship between the cliques and the whole group in its wider setting. From the point of view of Homans's systems theory, this means not realizing the constraints which the relationship with the wider setting has upon the cliques involved. A simple example of this occurred in the Bank Wiring Observation Room, where the competitiveness of cliques A and B was based upon what management expected of the group as a whole. Clique B wanted to annoy clique A *because* clique A met management's demands more closely; the extent of their competitiveness had to be contained within the bounds of the work which they had to complete each day.

From the point of view of studies which have looked at in-group favouritism, this criticism means not assuming that a group is simply a small number of people meeting together. The black recruit to the police force is a member of a racial group, even though he or she may be the only black person in uniform in the police station. This point has been laboured sufficiently already, but it goes to show that the word 'group' does not so much define a given number of individuals, as it indicates a state of social being, or a set of relationships. (It also indicates a state of mind, as we shall see below.)

There is another, contrasting view of groups which is raised by the work on multiple-group membership. This has been put forward recently by John Turner and his associates (Turner 1987), in what they call a *self-categorization theory*. This explanation hinges on the idea that people see themselves as being part of a group, so that they categorize themselves as part of 'this in-group' as opposed to 'that out-group'. This emphasis upon self-categorization is set against explanations, like that of Homans, which see groups arising out of the interactions of their members. In a series of experiments Turner and his colleagues found that, while social attraction leads people to see themselves as part of one group, self and other categorization is sufficient for this to occur even without members being attracted to one another. Put more simply, the argument is that people act together as a group through a recognition of similarities which they hold in common, not because they all like each other or spend time with each other. Turner and his associates present evidence from experiments which show that people can distinguish between acting on the basis of personal attraction, and acting on the basis of allegiance to a group to which they feel they belong. There seems little basis to doubt that people can make this distinction, and I shall elaborate upon the need for explanations of social interaction to encompass people's views of themselves in relation to others. The further point which Turner makes is that social identity should not be reduced to a feeling of 'selfhood' deriving from the individual as such. Instead, who one is, and the kind of person one might become are potentialities made possible only by the fact that these categories are socially shared. Being a Scotsman, or a Christian Scientist or a lesbian, provides identities for those concerned, not only because other people in their groups hold these ideas, but because these social categories are more generally shared in society as a whole.

The intersection of group affiliations

People are members of several groups at one time, a fact that has not always been recognized in the study of social relationships. In this section I want to develop this point to show its importance for explanations of how people act in groups. We have already seen that appearances and roles rely less upon individual differences than upon social distinctions. Now we need to appreciate the way in which these social distinctions have a bearing upon how individuals think and act as members of groups in society.

Let us begin with an imaginary situation, of a woman in her forties who has entered higher education once her children have left school. She finds herself in the company of men and women some years her junior, in age and in experience. In discussions during classes she notes that, when there are disagreements between the young men and the young women, she finds it difficult at times to know which side to support. For when it comes to some topics she identifies herself with the other women, while at the same time recognizing the motivations of the young men. She does this because they are not much older than her own sons, for whom (as a mother) she has a natural concern. Seeing two sides of the problem is at first an obstacle to her speaking her mind on the topic, but the counter-arguments presented and her attempts to think them through lead her to stating her own position. For in the end she is an equal member of an educational grouping, and as such ought to say what she thinks. In doing so she risks pleasing neither the other women nor the young men in the group; however, she might please the tutor.

This illustrates the fact that individuals are not just members of different groups but live at the intersections of the various groups to which they belong. In one sense the word 'intersection' is inaccurate, for it suggests a passive crossing point. In fact, this is not the case, as can be appreciated from the illustration used above. A consideration of what multiple-group membership in society means for people shows that this can help them to become aware of possibilities of which they were not conscious before.

An analysis of multi-group membership was carried out by the sociologist Georg Simmel (1955), in a now well-known essay, *Conflict and the Web of Group Affiliations*. From its title one can imagine the picture which Simmel had of social life, where the groups to which people belong constitute a system of co-ordinates which define them. He argued that with each new grouping that we join, we are defined more definitely. This is a source both of enrichment through expanded interests, and of tension through intensified conflict. Consider what happens when people get married or announce their intention of doing so. Although there is a general acceptance that this will involve the man and woman in abstaining from sexual relations with other members of the opposite sex, it also has implications for their relationships with members of their own sex. While it would be mistaken to pretend that these are the same in different social groups, there are nevertheless certain activities which unmarried men, for example, enjoy because they are free of marital ties. The 'stag party' before a man's wedding is a ritual celebrating (or should one say bemoaning) the loss of 'freedom' which he has until then enjoyed with his friends. When people of either sex get married, there is the question of whether their spouse (in our terms, the incipient family group) will 'allow' them to continue to be members of their old friendship groups. While this example is so familiar as to be a hoary old chestnut, it should not disguise the fact that getting married places special constraints on how those individuals can act in other groups of which they are members.

The fact that people are, or might be, members of other groups can in itself affect how their own group members act towards them. While external status characteristics were introduced earlier as if they were aspects of people's pasts which they brought with them to a new group, this is not necessarily the case. How does a family respond to the prospect of a parent's decision to enrol as a student at the Open University? What will it mean to have a graduate in the family? If a group of friends discovers that one of their number is to join the police force, what might be their response? In each case, the group members are anticipating that the individual's status in the new group will contradict or challenge his or her status in the old group. What if mum is too busy studying to cook the evening meal? What will our new PC friend do if we go out for a drink and have one too many? Not only are groups concerned with who may join their number, they are equally concerned with what their existing members might choose to become.

Simmel used the example of journeymen in the Middle Ages who were dissuaded, where possible, from getting married. If they did so, difficulties were placed in their way in future. The reason for this was that marriage restricted the migration of journeymen, an essential part of their livelihood, and undermined the independence of the group from its masters. The claims of groups to uphold certain standards or to have their membership regarded in a certain way, depends upon their preserving particular relationships with other key groupings. In the terms used by Goffman (1971), particular impressions are fostered by the group actively dissuading its members from participating in other groupings whose claims contradict those of 'the team'. In British politics, MPs who are members of the Labour Party are discouraged from having business connections which could suggest a misplaced interest in profits or social influence.

Simmel's analysis of multiple group membership is partly an historical one, but this does not make it less relevant for our purposes. He points out that from the Middle Ages onwards there was a movement towards the establishment of groupings based upon interests above those of the family, locale or traditional social position. The formation of medieval knighthood brought the nobility, freemen and vassals together in an association in which they were bound as equals under one standard of judgement. In a similar way, the emergence of groups of scholars transcends boundaries of privilege and nationality. This does not mean that external-status characteristics vanished from these groupings, nor that the new groups did not establish their own structures and hierarchies. These are things which we have already seen demonstrated in the social psychological studies reviewed. Within groups of scholars, for example, there emerged differences between them based upon the demands of the environment and of their own organization. Some would make original and highly valued contributions, others would become influential in the academic community. However, these differences were based upon criteria different to those which separated them in the groups to which they originally belonged. An individual, therefore, knew himself (more rarely herself) within both of these schemes and could evaluate one in terms of the other. Simmel's argument is that the emergence of multiple-group membership was instrumental in establishing the modern individual as a particular kind of social being, giving form to the way of thinking which underlies our assumptions of what it means to be a person today.

Simmel's argument is important to us in this book for two reasons. First, it critically undermines the idea that social interaction can be understood (except in the most superficial sense) by studying the exchanges of individuals taken outside their social settings. Social relationships are more than the meeting of personalities, and their establishment depends upon more than the smooth, efficient and friendly communication of feelings and ideas. When people act as group members, they do so in the knowledge of the groups to which they belong; this is the point made by the social-categorization theorists. Simmel's argument leads us to a position more embracing than this; when people act, they do so against the background of their membership in several groups whose relationship to each other is of direct relevance to understanding the interactions of the people concerned.

Multiple groups and the question of formality

Can we use these ideas on multiple-group membership to deepen our understanding of relationships in a particular group? This section describes one example of this, using concepts which we have already met in the analysis of the single group. The example is taken from an analysis made by Homans (1951) in his discussion of formality in relationships within the family. It has also formed the basis of an argument put forward for extending Bales's ideas to the family group. About the latter prospect, we have already made some critical remarks. We shall now examine this particular example to see the scope which individuals have for establishing relationships of different degrees of formality.

The problem is set within a comparison drawn originally by anthropologists studying family groupings in different cultures. On the island of Tikopia in the South Seas the relationship between a son and his father is one of respect, rather than close affection. Sons must work in the fields with their father and obey his authority. The relationship of the boy to his mother's brother is, by comparison, more equal, the 'uncle' (our terms for family relatives do not quite apply) showing in a friendly manner how the boy should cope with the difficulties which he will meet during his childhood and youth. Where the father is an authority figure to the boy, his mother's brother is a companion and guide to life's enigmas.

A direct contrast is shown in the case of a Melanesian culture, the Trobrianders, where the descent group is matrilineal rather than patrilineal. This means that, unlike the Tikopians (or Western society), the child's kin group is traced through the mother's line, not the father's. One consequence of this is that, as the male child grows up, he is expected to go and work under the direction of his mother's brother. There he will help till the fields, part of the crop produced going to his mother in return. The boy no longer works for his father, but the latter is helped in his fields by his own sister's sons. Therefore, where the basic unit of production in the Tikopia is made up of a man and his sons, in the Trobriands it is made up of a man and his sister's children. What is particularly interesting about this is that, where the boy in Tikopia has a relationship of respect and formality with his father, in the Trobriands this relationship is one of companionship. 'Father is all solicitude; the mother's brother is the instigator of the procedure by which the sister's son is shamed or disgraced for some misdeed.' (Homans 1951). The reason for this is that the father is released from exercising authority and control over his son, thus freeing him to indulge his affection for him. The two situations give rise to relationships which can be seen to be mirror opposites of one another.

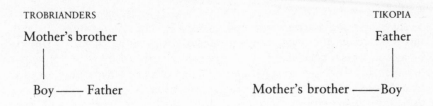

From Homans's point of view, this illustrates very well the influence of the external upon the internal system. The formality of the father–son relationship is not to be sought in biological endowment or in 'natural' feelings for one another, but in the limits which are placed upon them by the way the group meets the demands of the environment. Relationships of authority leave little room for affection; for that reason, bonds of affection grow elsewhere, with intimates who can show and lead without the need to demonstrate control.

An interesting gloss was put on this cultural difference in an attempt to relate it to Bales's ideas. Zelditch (1956) drew the same distinctions as above, but added that one should not assume that, because the father in the Trobriands does not exercise authority over his sons, his role is less instrumental in the home. For this man also has a sister, who has sons of her own. As they grow up they will help him in his fields, so that he will exercise authority over them. In both of the cultures considered, to the extent that a man is a father *and* a sister's brother, he will know relationships of greater and of lesser control, of easier and more difficult displays of affection. As already pointed out, marriage is the elaboration of kinship, so that to be at the intersect of two families is to enjoy (and suffer) the different statuses and demands of each grouping.

Zelditch argued that to understand this arrangement of roles we need to look beyond the nuclear family to its intersection with the descent grouping. (The key difference between the Tikopia and the Trobrianders was, to remind the reader, whether the line of descent was patrilineal or matrilineal.) The argument runs as follows. Where the nuclear family is relatively strong, and the descent group is weak (true for technological societies), then tasks will be formally carried out by fathers and sons in the nuclear family, and their relationship will tend to be marked by authority on one side and by respect on the other. Where, however, the descent group is relatively strong (as in the Trobriands), then tasks will be formally allocated within this structure, allowing for more informal relationships within the nuclear family. The essence of this claim, consistent with the position put forward by Simmel, is that the interactions within a group cannot be properly understood without appreciating its relationships with intersecting groupings.

Some remarks need to be made in order to place the above ideas in context. I am not suggesting that all relationships can easily be described in terms similar to those used above to compare the Tikopians and the

Trobrianders. Certainly the idea of intersecting groupings is one that has received little attention in social psychology to date. As mentioned above, this is the result of having treated groups of people either as little islands of humanity, or else of having focused exclusively upon the relationship of two (competing or co-operating) groups, the members of which are deemed to be exclusively defined by that group membership. This inevitably makes it difficult to consider the conflicts of interest which arise in everyday life from being a member, simultaneously, of several groups. However, in a world in which this condition is the norm, so that individuals may freely attach themselves to and disengage from one group after another, there is an increased potential for them to use their background experience to claim future status. The more people rise to sort out the conflicts with which they are faced, the more adept they might be at exploiting this experience in order to create 'impressions' of themselves. Arguably, there is a relationship between the need to manage a number of conflicting roles and the mental flexibility required to fashion one's identity for other people (Coser 1975).

Perspectives and the social self

So far, this chapter has dealt more with the fact of multiple group membership than with its consequences for social identity. This latter term refers to the idea that individuals identify themselves with, and sometimes as, particular sections of society. To think of oneself as 'working-class', 'a feminist', or as 'a devout Catholic' are expressions of social identity. These terms matter not just because people *think* of themselves in this way (although this is important), but also because they reflect the fact that people *act together* in such groups. A moment's reflection will show that these two facets of social life – thought and action – are not really separate but co-exist. We could say that people are able to act together because they think in similar terms, and that they think in these ways because of their experience of acting together. The point of raising this 'chicken and egg' dilemma is to show that the ways in which people interact are expressions of both structured groups and conscious minds. We are able to take part in social life because, in some important way, we understand it; the groups to which we belong, if not society as a whole, are somehow 'inside us'. Put in this blunt way this idea may seem unhelpful, but it does direct our attention to the need to say what kind of a person is able to take part in the full complexity of social relationships. There can be no full understanding of social interaction without some idea as to what the individuals who take part are like. In fact, everyday assumptions about 'the individual', like those about 'society', underlie all the research which social scientists undertake. By examining some proposals about what kind of being the 'social self' is, we obtain a critical view of the role of thought and feeling in everyday relationships. When one speaks of people who feel that they 'ought' to do this or 'choose to break the rules', what kind of psychological theory of mental life does this imply?

One theory which offers a comprehensive view of these matters was put forward some time ago by the American social philosopher G.H. Mead (1934). Mead wrote out his ideas over a period of time, and they were only collected together after his death. For many students today, Mead's theory does not make easy reading, but his proposals are still relevant to current issues in social psychology. Because of the sweep of his interests, this section can only sketch in those of his ideas which are of most use to us in this introduction to the topic. The keystone of the theory is a capacity which Mead does assume is uniquely human: the ability for a person to 'step inside the shoes' of someone else and see the world from that person's point of view. This does not mean that people are aware of doing this; in fact, many of the misunderstandings which arise between people happen precisely because they do not see the other's point of view! Mead's point is that it happens at a different level, being the basis of how we think and act in relation to one another.

If you think of 'standing in another person's shoes', say by imagining how someone you know well sees other people, then you will also get some picture of yourself as that other person sees you. And because you have that image – say you appear to yourself as 'gullible' in the eyes of the other person – then you have a response to that image and may, for example, decide to 'be more firm' with that person in the future. The ability, in Mead's terms, to 'take the attitude of the other' provides you with a perspective on yourself, so that you have a sense of yourself from that person's point of view. This self-image is then there as evidence of what the other person thinks of you, and what you in turn make of that appearance. For Mead, social relationships are possible only because we are able to take the attitude of others towards ourselves. We can then realize what is expected of us and be able to meet (or not to meet) these expectations in our dealings with them.

However, Mead's theory of social relations goes beyond the idea of taking the attitudes of individuals, of seeing things from the standpoint of a particular person. As a member of a group a person has to know both what particular others think and what he or she should do in order to play his or her part as a member. Mead was fond of using teams as examples of what he meant by this. In a football team, each player must understand his position and play in relation to that of others, in terms of a strategy and set of rules shared by the whole team. The strategy and rules correspond to what we might call 'an understanding of how the team plays its football', and is a general rather than a specific perspective which the player takes towards himself. The perspective is not only general, it is abstract, by which is meant that it applies to the team rather than to who is playing on any particular day. Also it is a shared perspective, a view of themselves as a collective which unites the players in a common view of who they are and what each expects of the others. Mead's term for this shared perspective is the 'generalized other', a label meant to indicate that the perspective is indeed an abstract one, and also that it appears, in experience, like another person. This last point is important and I shall take it up in a moment. First, it is important to see the implications of Mead's 'generalized other' for understanding social relationships.

Earlier in this chapter, I said that acting in a group inevitably involves people in knowing themselves as constituting a group (the social-categorization theory). The idea of an abstract perspective in Mead's theory is intended to serve this function, to explain how people act and think of themselves as part of a collective whole. Sometimes he spoke of the 'attitude of the group' to mean the same thing. There are familiar examples in all walks of life. Members of sports teams talk of 'how the team ought to play', and members of groups at work speak of there being 'low morale in the team'. Looking outwards, as it were, this perspective signifies the collectivity, the boundedness of the group in relation to other groupings. Looking inwards, towards the individual, it has a psychological function, in describing his or her place in relation to that collectivity.

When a person takes the attitude of the group, he or she thereby sees himself/herself from that perspective. In experience, formulated as a standpoint, it appears like an 'other' who indicates the person's position. For example, a member of the Communist Party will think, 'As a communist, it appears to me that . . .' and 'as a communist, I should do such and such . . .'. Readers can substitute for 'communist' in the sentence any group label which they wish, especially names of groups of which they are members. In every case, the group concerned has its own perspective on the world, as part of which is its claim upon the individuals who are its members. The 'generalized other' is a standpoint which each group member can take and, in so doing, each of them indicates to himself/herself the group's expectations, values and ideals. Looking 'outwards', the concept indicates an objective collectivity, a group of people which meets regularly to do specific things, having its own history and ideology; looking 'inwards' the concept describes the definition of self which that perspective indicates, the sense of social identity which is produced.

The above ideas reflect Mead's wider concern to create a theory of social life in which the 'self', the conscious person, is integral with the social group. By 'integral with' I mean that he saw selves and society as two sides of the same coin. Why be concerned with this point in a book about social relationships? The reason is very simple, once we acknowledge it. It is that how people think they might act in their dealings with each other is inextricably tied up with their participation in such groupings. To return to the oversimplified statement of the problem expressed previously, somehow society 'gets inside' individuals, and individual intentions 'steer' society. For Mead, there could be no society as we know it without self-conscious individuals, *thinking, feeling* people; there could be no such individuals without a society of differentiated groupings which had an objective existence. It is not just that particular people categorize themselves as being members of specific groups, for these groups exist in the world. In their products and in their possessions different social groups fashion an objective environment which helps to sustain their existence. Doctors do not exist as a group only because a sufficiently large number of individuals think of themselves in this way and are thought of as such by the remainder of society. The medical perspective is a way of thinking indeed, but it is also the organization of health care in all its different forms, including the technical and the physical arrangements for that care to be delivered (e.g. hospitals).

Mead saw people as doing more than just taking one abstract attitude towards themselves. They take many perspectives according to the various groups to which they belong. What allows people to act as members of their local community is their capacity to take on an attitude of sufficient generality. This means that there needs to be some organization of perspectives within the person, so that, for example, people can act as 'citizens of the state' when called upon to sit on a jury. The idea of acting as a citizen is an invitation to transcend the specific differences between social groupings, so that we should not judge a man guilty because he is a different skin colour than ourselves, or find a woman at fault because her manner does not fit our conception of how women should act. From what we have seen of evidence about jury groups, this idea has more of the ring of an ideal to it than actual observation. Indeed, Mead's apparent concern to fit the individual with the community as a whole has led several critics to draw attention to the limitations of this view. Why, for example, should members of minority groups or of disadvantaged sections of society take on an attitude which presents all people as having a common interest in the community?

Instead, we may take the view that people are members of groups which do not always have things in common and may often be in competition for resources. In that case, being a member of several such groups will lead individuals to experience themselves from these different perspectives. This idea should not be taken on lightly, for it gives the impression that a world of multiple groups is simply reflected in the individual as a multiplicity of selves. As we shall see below, there is more to the idea of the 'social self' than this. For the moment, we can relate Mead's view to the proposals of Simmel, for whom the membership of several groups requires people to confront the contradictions with which they are faced. For example, by taking the perspective of the family towards themselves adolescents are aware of their duties to their parents; however, by taking the perspective of their friendship group they are aware of themselves as young adults who have certain expectations of deciding their own future. In the realms of career, or of courtship, these perspectives may within individual experience contradict one another. Then individuals may feel that they are 'two different selves', so that they need to be one thing in one situation and something else in another. In spite of this, Mead argues that to be a self, to be a unique personality with an identity, there must be some organization of these competing perspectives. To explore this claim further, we need to know something of Mead's proposals about how people act as self-conscious individuals.

Self-consciousness and social action

The 'generalized other' is an awareness of ourselves from the perspective of the group; it is to think *like* a group member, as well as to think of oneself *as* a group member. For example, when one becomes a parent, one takes a perspective through which things in the environment appear that are either dangerous or potentially of interest to children. These things one may never have noticed before, nor cared too much about them when other people pointed them out. Interestingly enough, these new awarenesses often arise for people when they hear that they are to become a parent for the first time. This shows that, to take the perspective of a group, one does not have to be a fully paid-up member. The term reference group is intended to cover our identifications both with groups to which we actually belong and participate in, and those groups to which we would like one day to belong, or with which we have sympathy. So, for example, fit people can espouse the cause of the handicapped, whites can argue for equal rights for black people, and the most modest home can display a picture of the Royal Family as an expression of support for the monarchy. From what was said earlier in this chapter about the definition of common interests by unequal groups, it is inevitable that individuals embrace the possibility of the opposing group's perspective, even though they may rarely step into its shoes, so to speak. In Britain every member of the Conservative Party has an implicit understanding of the Labour Party's position and vice versa. This under-standing may be superficial, it may be distorted as seen by the group in question, but it is there as a counter-support to the individual's own political persuasion.

Mead attempted to describe the way in which people think through their actions by reference to his concept of the 'self' which involves two inseparable but qualitatively different aspects. These he termed the 'I' and the 'me'. The use of inverted commas around these terms is important, because it shows that they do not refer to things inside people but to aspects of their experience. At its simplest, the 'I' is our experience of ourselves as we are acting; the 'me' is the image of ourselves when we reflect upon what we did do or could do. Let us return to the example given when describing the generalized other; a man might wonder what he should do, 'as a member of the Communist Party'. The 'me' which he is aware of at the time is that aspect of himself involved in politics of a certain kind. Perhaps he will do one thing, or say another, but however he acts on the basis of his view of himself as a communist, he grasps this as something that *he* does, as an 'I'. Only as the thinker or the actor is there available to us this fleeting sense of ourselves as the authors of our own lives.

This example makes certain points about Mead's analysis which are not easy to appreciate. Notice that the 'me' does not refer to a consciousness of the whole person in the abstract; it is *situated*, by which social scientists mean that it derives from the person's place in the world. Second, the 'I' is not some mysterious inner or 'real' part of the personality but the person acting. We can compare the 'I' to Goffman's concept of self as *performer*, and the 'me' to the self as *character*. For Mead these two aspects of the social self are complementary and inseparable. To be part of a group we must have some awareness of things from the group perspective; to act in the group we must be able to answer the demands of the group as we perceive them.

There is an implied circularity in the relationship of the 'I' and the 'me'. 'I' act on the basis of my perception of what should, could or ought to be done ('me'), and as a result become aware of myself ('me') in relation to what was intended in my actions ('I'). Although people act upon the basis of the perspective of the group ('me'), this should not be seen as determining what they do ('I'). A person's action, whether it be to kick at a football, to proffer a hand, or to make an amusing contribution in a tutorial, cannot be wholly determined or predicted. There is an essential openness about social life, in spite of the fact that it is guided and understood in terms of expectations which the abstract perspectives provide. The 'should, may and ought' of the 'generalized other' define the possibilities for action, but they cannot prescribe what will actually occur. This is in spite of the fact that self-consciousness enables us to think through and to plan what we might do. Even rehearsing what will be said at the right moment, to someone expecting your words, does not guarantee that things will work out as anticipated. Tolstoy makes one of his characters, Koznyshev, determine to propose marriage to Varenka who willingly anticipates his proposal as they collect mushrooms together in a wood:

Now or never was the moment for his declaration – Koznyshev felt that, too. Everything about Varenka, her expression, the flushed cheeks and downcast eyes, betrayed painful suspense. He saw it and felt sorry for her. He even felt that to keep silent now would be to wrong her. He quickly ran over in his mind all the arguments in support of his decision. He even repeated to himself the words in which he had intended to put his offer, but instead of those words some perverse reflection caused him to ask:

'What is the difference between a white boletus and a birch mushroom?'

Varenka's lips trembled with agitation as she replied:

'There is hardly any difference in the top part, but the stalks are different.'

As soon as these words were out of her mouth, both he and she understood that it was over, that what was to have been said would not be said, and their excitation, having reached its climax, began to subside.

(Anna Karenin)

This view of the relationship between the 'I' and the 'me' is also consistent with the idea of impressions formed from information 'given off' and 'given'. While social identity is bound up with group membership and with expectations of what should be done, its expression in action is only completed in terms of the outcome of what we do. I may try to give a particular impression, I may intend to portray a particular side to my character or I might endeavour wholeheartedly to fulfil the expectations of the group to which I belong. Trying, intending and endeavouring may not, however, be enough, although they are a vital part of the manner in which social life is expected to be lived. However, the 'slippage' between these dual features of the self is far from being a limitation to explanations of social relationships. Many significant judgements which are made about people are in terms of the effort which they have or have not made, not just the outcome of their actions (Jones and deCharms 1958). Courage, tenacity, weakness and cowardice refer not to outcomes but to the responses of individuals to what other people have expected of them.

The picture which Mead gives us of the social self is one of individuals who act with a consciousness of their role in society. The perspectives which they assume and adopt provide them with outline schemes which, running ahead of experience, define and guide it (Shibutani 1955). The multiple groups to which people belong present them with alternative perspectives, organized to be a system of choices of possible action. As people may adopt the perspective of groups to which they aspire, and as they can consider alternatives to acting in the way they should behave in their social settings, they have the capacity to *imagine* how to be different. The ability to adopt an alternative perspective makes it possible to say, 'What if I acted like this?', or 'What would they think if I was to do such and such?' The capacity to 'act as if' opens up a range of potential ways of acting, from full-blown pretence to modifications in one's usual style of conduct (Radley 1978). So a person can say, 'If I am just a little more confident next time, then perhaps . . .', indicating an awareness of one's own action as it affects the other person. Mead's theory does not require people to dramatize their roles in the way that Goffman (1971) suggests is often necessary, but it provides an account of the social self in which this potential is latent.

5

PLAYFULNESS AND SERIOUSNESS

The theme for this chapter is the degree to which people act in a serious or playful manner, colouring their actions so as to convey either commitment or lightheartedness. This is not an arbitrary choice of topic, because it raises issues concerning the very nature of what passes between people in the course of social life. In particular, it concerns how we come to feel that someone is 'real' and 'true', rather than 'pretending' or 'cynical'. What matters in our dealings with each other are things that we say we really mean – 'Oh, yes, when I looked him in the eye and said, "I'm going to leave you," he knew that I was in earnest.' Taking things seriously, being in deadly earnest, playing the fool, making a mockery of someone, all refer to ways of doing things of which we approve or disapprove. They are also, in one sense, judgements about the people concerned, so that, for example, one might conclude that the person is 'a bit stupid' because he treats everything as if it were a joke.

In relation to appearances, the theme of playfulness/seriousness is one dimension along which individuals can express themselves and make particular impressions upon others. Indeed, far from being just one dimension, I shall argue that this theme colours all of people's social activity and is a key issue in the successful claiming of identities by individuals. The appropriateness of acting in an informal way depends not only upon the situation, but also upon the expected ways of behaving of the group concerned. A group of friends out for the evening or taking a weekend trip to the coast will treat the outing as an opportunity to 'let their hair down' and have a bit of fun. How easily the group does this will depend upon its structure, as it will upon the readiness of particular individuals to play the fool at every opportunity. Formality and informality are characteristics which are appropriately applied to the group context. In the previous chapter a picture of the social self was drawn which showed that actions (and words) do not simply happen but are the attempt by individuals to fulfil expectations or to convey ideas to other group members. This capacity for self-conscious action provides the basis for people to stand apart from what is expected of them. When discussing these matters in the context of appearances and expressions, we saw that making a successful claim meant persuading someone of one's sincerity and legitimate claim to the role in question, be it 'bright student' or 'cool customer'. Now we shall see that this is only one way of establishing an impression. The reason for this can be found in our discussion of the multiplicity of groups to which we belong; we do not always want to be identified with what we do, nor do we always want to be taken entirely seriously in all matters attaching to our name.

Role distance: the merry-go-round

In an essay called *Role distance*, Erving Goffman (1961) introduced his analysis with a brief discussion of that well-known fairground attraction, the merry-go-round. In a form reminiscent of Homans's analysis, he argued that the merry-go-round can be seen as a system whose basic unit of activity (the technical arrangement of the ride) is transformed by the orientation of the riders to the situation. As the ride gets under way, this orientation is expressed by the shifts in feeling and behaviour of the riders, and in particular the extent to which they show themselves involved. Anyone who has stood and watched a merry-go-round will have seen that there is, in fact, a variety of riders. Most, as one would expect, are children; some are parents accompanying their children while a few are teenagers or young adults enjoying the fun. Goffman says that we should not just think of the merry-go-round rider as occupying a single role. Indeed, looking at the riders, we can see that they do not all take to the prospect in the same way. Some small children, who wanted so much to get on, positively fight their parents to get off before it begins. Once it is under way, others are to be seen gripping their steeds tightly in order to organize the muscular control necessary both for staying physically secure, and for proving that they are old enough to ride alone. For them, the excitement of the ride is mixed in equal quantity with fear of falling off, so that riding the wooden horse demands all of their attention. With a little more experience these small children will let go with one hand to risk a small wave to their parents who are watching, showing that they are not just riding but are enjoying doing so. Older children, on the other hand, are to be seen treating the ride in a cavalier fashion, tapping their feet to the music, patting the horse's head, leaning back while hanging on to the pole. As Goffman puts it, this is as if to say: 'Whatever I am, I'm not just someone who can barely manage to stay on a wooden horse.' This attitude creates a distance between the image which the child would have if he or she were merely to ride the wooden horse, and the self which is created by this skittish behaviour. This is what Goffman calls *role distance*, a concept which he uses to analyse the ways in which people affect, alter and manipulate the roles which they occupy in order to fashion some preferred image of themselves.

This idea is made clearer by considering merry-go-round riders who are of or near adult age. Goffman says that for 12-year-old boys, the need to show role distance (i.e. not to be seen by the watchers as merely riding the horse) is acute, but the means for them to achieve this are not easy. They have to make the ride into a lark, a mockery in order that they should distance themselves from it. Unlike the 8-year-old who obtains a thrill from the nonchalant manner of his or her participation, the teenager has to produce elaborate and daring additions to make his or her participation into 'fun'. Adults who mount the merry-go-round also adopt role-distancing manoeuvres, although these need to be less dramatic. Goffman gives the example of the young lady who calls out to her watching boyfriend 'Come on, don't be chicken.' Finally, who has not noticed the nonchalant manner of the adult who operates the ride? He moves about the merry-go-round with ease, getting on and off while it moves, and standing without support while taking the customers' money. Through this he shows that, for him, the ride is not 'a ride' at all; it is not an event but a routine part of his working life.

Goffman argues that role distancing is something people do when they are placed in positions which they feel are somewhat beneath the status with which they credit themselves. This explains the behaviour of the older boys on the merry-go-round. However, it also applies to some men in the way that they help with the housework or with the shopping, particularly when in the sight of some of their male friends. Then they may adopt a careful clumsiness in the cleaning or confess to a total ignorance of the whereabouts of goods in the supermarket. Parents who help out at their children's school fêtes show, by 'hamming it up', their disaffection for the role of persuading people to try to throw table-tennis balls into small glass jars for prizes of dubious value. At other times, such as when trying out an activity for the first time, people sometimes make a mockery of it in order to avoid the criticism which is levelled at someone who properly fills the role. The girl who lets out a series of alternating laughs and screams as she wobbles on the sailboard may be having fun, and being apprehensive at the same time, but through her cavorting she is communicating not ineptitude, but a lack of commitment to the role of sailboarder. This does not guarantee that watchers on the beach will not see her as unskilled, or even as frightened, but they cannot judge her as failing to carry out expertly an activity which she does not claim to take seriously. From the girl's point of view, this role distance means that she too can feel herself less committed, and that it is only an act. (However, as we saw in chapter 2 in the excerpt from Jules Feiffer's play, just because we put on an act does not guarantee that others will not accuse us of being *really* what we seem.)

Other examples of role distance include those shown by subordinates required to carry out orders with which they do not wish to comply; the shopgirl asked to tidy the counter does it casually and while biting her nail, or the boy who is told by his mother to wash his hands before dinner slouches to the bathroom in front of his friend. In these cases, it is the presence of other people who might see them as really occupying these roles which is important. One does not wish to be seen as a 'henpecked husband' or a 'downtrodden shopgirl' any more than as a rider of merry-go-round horses. Goffman provides further examples of this kind in the case of surgical interns who are completing their medical training. Through their actions (leaning on the anaesthetized patient, putting a foot on an upturned bucket), they convey that their presence in theatre is not to be taken as a sign of their commitment to a career in surgery. This is the eternal danger of doing a job precisely and no more, that one will be taken as 'nothing but that role', and therefore have attributed to you those qualities of co-operation, deference and dependability which add up to being taken for granted. We are less likely to be seen in terms of our individual personalities the more closely we fit the image of someone who fills that particular position or role (Jones, Davis and Gergen 1961). As we have seen in chapter 3, the way that people adapt what must be done (be it wooden-horse riding, lathe operating or giving a seminar paper) depends upon the norms of the group. So, for example, on the shop floor it might be the 'done thing' to operate one's machine with the safety guard up while paying only partial attention to one's work. In the seminar group one's friends do not expect a thirty-minute delivery, being the distillation of careful note-taking and consideration. By all means be bright, but above all be witty!

Role distancing is not employed in every situation. In chapter 2, when introducing Goffman's work on impression making, it was pointed out that one of the ways in which people establish their claims to be a particular kind of person or to occupy a role is through dramatic realization. This would appear to be the opposite of role distancing because the person attempts to convey an air of total involvement in the activity. The two are similar, however, in both involving the person in a dramatic enactment, in one case aimed at a consistency of all aspects of the performance, and in the other at a contrived disparity between some aspects of the role performance and others. In the case of role distancing, Goffman argues that it serves the function of showing to other people that the individuals in question do not embrace totally the role that they find themselves in, while they hold all other roles in abeyance. In a world of multiple-group membership, there are positive gains to be had from showing others that the relationship with them is not one's only or even one's prime involvement. What some people call 'sophistication' is precisely the affectation of dis-involvement which is meant to indicate that the person is somehow above any particular role or position in which others try to place him or her. Life becomes all style and no substance. (In fact, this affectation is adopted most successfully by people who do have substantial means at their disposal, i.e. the rich and famous.)

From the earlier discussion of role differentiation in groups it seems unlikely that role distancing is the prerogative of the subordinate. We have seen that people who have higher status in groups exercise greater discretion as to how to behave, and Goffman confirms this, using the example of surgical teams. Here the senior staff make small jokes and use informalities in ways which relax the *status quo*. While subordinates distance themselves in order to show some independence from the strictures of a relationship, those in charge do this in order to demonstrate their 'human qualities', or their social graces. They have the power not only to make others obey, but also to create moments of levity and of apparent equality among the people in the room. And on weekends they may adopt clothes of a rough and ready kind which belies their status and income, so that they may be seen not only as successful people, but as important individuals to whom one may talk about football or the kinds of vegetables to grow in one's garden.

The concept of role distance is a useful one with which to begin this chapter because it shows the difference between *playing* a role (where people are identified with what they do) and *playing at* a role, where the impression gained of them depends upon their ability to be in the situation but not of it. This ambiguity should not be seen as some kind of extra to the apparently more serious job of fulfilling the demands of one's role, because it is positively expected by others within our social groups. The concept of the internal system and the idea of the social-emotional leader in the group assume that certain members will be able to make light of disputes. They are the ones to make jokes or play around and, by setting aside their authority for a moment, have an informal influence which group members come to expect and to accept. In this chapter we are having a closer look at how these things are done, and at the implications of these ideas for our study of social relationships in general.

Excitement and reality: drama, ritual and routine

In the description of the merry-go-round we saw that the adoption of varying role distances by the riders made different impressions on the people watching them go round and round. This variation depends upon the age and (to a lesser extent) upon the ability of the rider. Small children find the ride both exciting and sometimes a little frightening, a feeling that older children and adults get from faster, steeper and higher rides, such as roller-coasters and 'corkscrews'. Even here, some might say especially here, teenage riders go to lengths to show (by holding their arms in the air) that they are not mere riders of the roller-coaster. The degree and the form of role distancing give us clues as to their experience, where the word experience means both 'how often the ride has been taken', and 'the feeling which the rider gets from doing it'. We can see this most easily by contrasting the small child who clings to the pole of his horse with the older child who plays around on it, and both of these with the man who operates the merry-go-round. For the small child the ride is a thrill concocted of excitement and a little fear, a small drama in his or her life. For the older child the ride is perhaps an experience taken annually, something which is done with friends together. As part of the pattern of their fairground experience it has a ritual quality, in demonstrating to each other their courage, imagination and disrespect for adult rules. For the operator the movement about the ride is a routine experience, a literal round of work comprising serious exchanges. These three terms, drama, ritual and routine, are introduced here to show that they (like the concept of social identity) point in two directions; outwards to differences in the social world, and inwards to differences in personal experience (Morris 1972). In this chapter we shall find that we need both of these aspects to account for variations in the seriousness with which people treat each other, and themselves also.

Sometimes one can see one of these aspects as dominant in a social situation; the drama of a road-traffic accident, the ritual of carving the Sunday roast, the routine of putting out the cat for the night. Further reflection, however, shows that social life is rarely, if ever, divisible into these separate categories, for several reasons. The excitement of the road accident is a drama for the victims and for the onlookers (though in quite different ways), but for the ambulance attendants it has certain routine qualities, for it is something which they do every day. More important, however, is the interweaving of these aspects which shows that it is a mistake to try to separate them absolutely. The ambulance personnel do not merely carry out routine tasks for the victims; although they employ technical skills, they do this in the context of a caring role which employs small rituals of consideration and respect for the victims. These rituals derive from the way people expect to be treated by strangers in everyday life ('Just a moment, dear, I'll cover up your legs there, you lie quietly, it will be all right.') This has the effect of rendering to the victim the kind of role distance which we have seen people claim for themselves, i.e. that even as one lies in the road, one is not treated merely as an accident victim, but as a person occupying other, more important, roles in life.

One person's drama is sometimes fashioned out of how other people play up their routines. The circus audience gasps as the high-wire act go through their routines, but the performers do this in a way which emphasizes the dangers and conceals some of the practised skills which they have acquired. One person's excitement is another person's daily experience, although in the case of the high-wire act a break in the routine can literally precipitate a crisis. Even here, there is an ambiguity in what people sense as real and as play or entertainment. Some members of the audience might perceive a fall into the net as 'part of the act', designed to amplify the danger to the crowd. People do not just vary the degree to which they play at occupying roles, but others know that they do so. This was illustrated in the case of one of the author's colleagues who, out jogging one day, fell over a lady's dog and badly twisted his knee. As he lay writhing on the ground, interspersed with pleas for her to help him, she remonstrated with him as a way of finding out if he was some kind of mugger. In this case, the problem for the jogger was to create the impression that his (real) agonies were real, and that this was a different kind of drama to the one which the lady thought might be in the offing.

We have seen in this section that roles *played* and roles *played at* can give a different impression to onlookers, but often constitute different experiences for the occupants concerned. There is a different sense of reality involved, so that the world and other people can have quite distinct feels to them as the situation varies. Dramas, rituals and routines depend upon one another, or should we say that under different situational demands people attempt to put these aspects together in different ways. The child clinging to the merry-go-round may be engaged in a relatively private drama, realized most acutely in the muscular tension of her body, this being the very routinized act upon which the ritual display of the teenage rider depends. In Homans's terms, we might say that the elaborate antics of the teenager feed back and transform the routines which were once learned in response to the need to stay on the wooden horse. Social life involves us in making out for others how serious or how playful are our engagements, whether it be fairground riding or asking someone for a date. In the following sections we shall examine further how this is achieved and what happens where it breaks down.

Ritual exchanges and ceremonies

Rituals and ceremonial behaviours develop in response to situations where the order of things is threatened by some transition, ambiguity, conflict or uncontrollable happening (Turner 1977). In the detail of social life, patterned exchanges of this kind occur when, for example, one person causes unintended offence to another.

'Ouch!' (withdrawing foot).
'Oh, I'm terribly sorry.'
'That's OK' (stops rubbing toe).
'Good' (smiles deferentially).

This example is similar to one used by Goffman (1972) to show how people establish or recover the respect which they grant themselves or the other person. The interchange is ritualistic in being made up of symbolic acts which signify the status of the people concerned. All rituals have this in common, no matter how they may vary; they communicate something about the status order in society. In order that they may do this, knowledge of ritual exchanges is shared by people, although this does not mean that all subscribe to them in the same way. That we expect people to share this knowledge is made apparent just by remembering the last time someone bumped into you in the street and passed on without a word.

The above exchange can be analysed by means of the terms which Goffman uses to explain what is happening in an interaction which is so commonplace as to seem banal. The order of events is as follows:

'*Ouch!*' This is a challenge and calls attention to the misconduct, tacitly invoking the rights of the injured party to have his or her dignity as a person recognized.

'*Oh, I'm terribly sorry.*' This is an offering to the person claiming injury and in effect acknowledges the obligation of the perpetrator to put things right. This move is a response within a range of possibilities which the offending party can adopt. In cases where someone's foot has been trodden on, the response often implies an unintended happening, but where it involves something said (and offence has been taken) the offering may claim that this was 'only a joke'. The removal of intent or of seriousness from the action defuses it of potential for creating offence.

'*That's OK.*' This is the acceptance of the offering and shows that the offended person accepts the other's claim that no offence was intended. Obviously, this particular response is not an inevitable one, for the person might feel that the other's offering is neither sufficiently sincere nor persuasive. ('Did I? Sorry.' or 'Really? I thought you were going the other way.')

'*Good.*' This is an expression of gratitude made by the offender to the other person in thanks for having let him or her off the hook. It usually signals the end of this particular exchange.

This analysis shows what can be revealed by treating very ordinary exchanges as rituals, having particular moves and rules which give them a definite form. We should note that this ritual occurs in response to a break in the routines of the people concerned (e.g. passing through a doorway) and yet involves an element of ambiguity. This ambiguity is not the cause of the ritual but is an inevitable consequence of its beginning. For there is no certainty as to the way that the people involved will play it. The offending person might say 'sorry', but he or she might say 'Watch where you're going.' This means that the actual status of the individuals is brought into question by the challenge and remains in doubt until, through the exchange, each is restored to his or her appropriate place. This is an important point, for it says that the ritual is not merely a homeostatic device, correcting deviations from the normal flow of events, but is the means by which those involved establish the social order in which they can then discuss other things. In other situations, where those concerned have minimal involvement with each other, the ritual may take the form of establishing superior status at the cost of any further communication. One has only to think of the exchange of rude gestures between motorists who are arguing over some element of their driving to see this occur.

The concept of ritual has a longer history in the work of the anthropologists who have described the many different ceremonies in which people engage to mark the transition of individuals from one status to another in a particular culture (Moore and Myerhoff 1977). When boys and girls reach puberty, there may be elaborate rituals which involve what are known as rites of passage. These rites are various, sometimes involving symbolic cutting of the body (as in circumcision) to mark both literally and metaphorically the admittance of the person to the ranks of the adults in the culture. In Western societies such rituals are more circumscribed and far less elaborate, being limited to a twenty-first birthday party and the giving of gifts symbolizing the young person's freedom from the authority of the parents (the 'key of the door'). Because the rituals of preliterate cultures often involve the whole tribe, or a substantial part of it, they are more publicly accessible in terms of observing the rites in which the principal actors engage. (Rites are the particular actions or words said as part of the ritual conducted. For example, as part of Holy Communion the priest offers the host (bread) to the supplicants.) However, just because an anthropologist can see someone doing a particular thing, this does not mean that he or she can understand the episode. One needs to know the significance of the words or gestures in order to understand the rules which govern the actions of all the different participants.

In Western culture the rituals which have the most explicit rule structure are those which we call ceremonies. These are formalized rituals in which particular people, each having a specified status in society, play particular roles in the performance of the rites involved. Where, above, we have just considered rituals as restoring breaks in the flow of social interaction, ceremonies appear as distinct episodes on their own. Examples include weddings, funerals and the Christmas festival.

Harré and Secord (1972) used Goffman's work as the basis for setting out a formal theory of social life based upon the understanding of all interaction in terms of rule-bound episodes. They took, as their ideal type, the formal episode, of which the wedding is a good example. The essence of this kind of analysis is to describe the rule structure within which the individuals concerned operate, to describe what ought, may or must be done in order that the ritual shall be considered complete. Let us follow their analysis a little way in order to see what it entails. The reason for doing this is to show one line of research which has flowed from Goffman's writings. It also illustrates the strengths and weaknesses of making the study of rules the central part of one's theory of social life. For we have already seen in the concept of role distance a powerful argument for playing *at* roles being as important as playing *out* roles in social interaction. How does this apply to the ceremony?

Taking the example of a wedding ceremony, Harré and Secord point out that its meaning resides in the doing of the acts which make it up. Although there are no specific guidelines on how each person should play his or her part, there is a liturgy which sets out what the marriage ceremony involves. The bride's father usually (and symbolically) 'gives her away', but someone else may fill this position if the bride's father cannot be present. The best man provides the ring, but there are no guidelines as to who should fill this position, only convention. What matters in the marriage ceremony is that the right words are said in the correct order by the appropriate people. It is this ordering of words and actions which constitutes the ritual, and which on completion makes the man and woman into husband and wife in the face of all present and of society as a whole. As Harré and Secord point out, minor variations in the execution of the rites do not affect the outcome (the bride's father may mutter, the best man has to substitute a curtain ring), and neither do the private thoughts and feelings of those taking part. The officiating priest may find the pair standing in front of him a rather unsavoury duo, the bride's mother may be wishing her daughter had chosen a different man, and the groom may be somewhat the worse for drink, but these things are not material to the effective dramatization of the ritual; the pair are married just the same.

For Harré and Secord the analysis of such formal ceremonies provides a model for understanding any situation in life as a kind of rule-bound episode. The key to understanding social life in this way is to realize that these are not substantive but symbolic exchanges. This difference has been illustrated by Goffman (1961) who contrasted the rules which we have about property ownership with those which apply when, say, people greet each other. In the case of property ownership, the rules are there to protect the rights of people concerning tangible goods; they are not there to signify things about the owners themselves. In the case of the formalities of saying hello and goodbye, the ritual exchanges have little or nothing to do with the content of the interaction, and everything to do with the conventions by which those concerned establish their identities and their worth for each other.

Greetings and partings are sometimes called 'access rituals'. To ask people on meeting them 'How are you?' is not to seek for factual (substantive) information about their health, but to initiate a relationship with them. Of course, there may be times when this question means precisely what it says, but then it is asked in such a way that its meaning is made distinct. One indication that the question is a symbolic move in a ritual exchange is that sometimes the questioner hardly waits for an answer but waves and passes on his or her way. As with the apology exchange described above, there is no fixed form to such interactions. What Goffman is showing us is the kind of thing we might learn if we treat social interaction *as if* it had the form of a ritual. It is not the cataloguing of the many and varied 'rituals' of social life that we are encouraged to undertake, but to see people as engaged in building and rebuilding the scaffolding of interactions as part of the expression of their identities. As an illustration, greetings and farewells punctuate social episodes by cutting through the ambiguity of where each one begins and ends. To watch people saying hello to each other is to see the variety of ways in which this can be done. Sometimes it is done reluctantly, as when two people would have preferred to pass by without acknowledging one another; at other times it is the elaborate and protracted greeting of a friend not seen for some time. A greeting expresses not only that a conversation will now take place, but what degree of conversation and for how long. Goffman notes that it is one of the signs of skilled co-operation that, as a group of friends take their leave of each other, it can be done in such a way that there is no explicit indication of who wished to go first, to curtail his or her time with the others. And finally, the symbolic meaning of the protracted goodbye to a friend who is to go away for some time (or for good) is nowhere made more poignant than in the chance meeting after the farewell has taken place; the relationship has been carefully closed and the other, so warmly despatched but recently, is best avoided.

Framing behaviour: a theory of playfulness in social relationships

This section deals primarily with playfulness in social relationships and only secondarily with play. The reason for this is that, when one looks closely, it becomes impossible to make a hard and fast division between the world of play and the world of serious behaviour. In everyday thinking, we do make this distinction when talking about work versus play, but these categories only indicate that we are distinguishing between areas of life in very broad terms. Play, apart from adult leisure activities, is usually thought of as the province of children and, no matter who does it, there are always connotations of childlike (or childish) behaviour when it is spoken about. Perhaps for this reason, social scientists who study interaction have paid little attention to play, being more concerned to discover the rules by which adults predict each other in the quest for accuracy or effectiveness of communication. However, as we shall see, playful elements in people's words and actions are so common as to make us rethink this question entirely, throwing new light on what we mean by serious action at the same time.

Think for a moment about situations when you have seen the following occur: teasing a friend, flirting with someone else's girlfriend/boyfriend, cheating in a friendly game of cards, making a sarcastic remark, making a threatening gesture, slapping someone on the back when you meet them. What these actions have in common is that they 'say something' in a way that is open to more than one interpretation. In each case the action does not mean what, if taken 'seriously', it would mean. The teasing is a criticism of the person's looks or character which is not to be taken as a real attack. If the person being baited gets angry and responds in fury, the others often laugh at him or her and say 'Can't take a joke?' Sarcasm is similar, in that the remark conveys a barb wrapped in the sugar paper of a smile, so that the victim may find it difficult to know how to respond. While the slap on the back might appear straightforward, there is always the question of how hard the slap can be before it seems to signal more than a greeting. In the Bank Wiring Observation Room study referred to in chapter 3, the method of bringing men into line on the norms for output rates was 'binging', a blow on the arm from another group member. This censure was a friendly warning from a fellow worker, but its coercive intent was never in question (Homans 1951).

These examples are not isolated pieces of experience, but representative of much of the way that people relate to one another. Much of the informal talk of people includes jokes and lighthearted comments, and in the world of work duties may be carried out in a way which shows that the person does not take these things too seriously. Social life is not made up of a series of 'words and blows' like beads on a string. The ambiguity in psychological life, to which I have pointed already, is nowhere more apparent than in those moments when we are 'just joking'.

Whether it is play, joking or sarcasm there is a need to signal to the other person that what one is saying (doing) or about to say, means something other than what the words (actions) literally mean. There must be some capacity for people to communicate on two levels simultaneously, so that the words (acts) are taken in the context intended. In fact, this capacity is not limited to humans alone, and the theory of playfulness we are about to consider was first conceived not in the consulting room or at the theatre, but in a zoo. Gregory Bateson (1987) noticed that, as monkeys played, they used a variety of signals which were similar to but not identical with combat (e.g. calls, lunges, bites and pulling at fur). There is sufficient difference between these signals that visitors to any zoo can tell (admittedly, not always) that animals are playing and not fighting. What Bateson noted was that the actions of the animals were changed in such a way that their meaning was transformed, though the original forms of the actions were still discernible. Put in another way, it meant that, when an animal nipped another, it was as if to say 'This nip which denotes a bite does not denote what a bite would normally denote.' In terms of examples from human communication this is the same as saying, 'This slap on the back (or insult) denotes a blow, but it does not mean what a blow (insult) would normally mean.'

This statement contains a paradox, by saying what is not intended and meaning what is not said openly. 'Good afternoon,' said to a colleague arriving in the office at 10.30 a.m., is not a misplaced greeting, but a comment upon his or her sense of responsibility with regard to the job. Play and joking have to be signalled, so that the other person knows how the communication to follow is to be taken. This is equally true for animals, who are quite capable of doing this (watch your family dog or cat for a demonstration). This means that the signal acts as a context or frame about the actions done or the words spoken. Bateson refers to this as a *metacommunication*, meaning a message above or about the message being sent. In face-to-face relationships this invariably involves some use of the body or tone of voice, so that the physical attitude of the person, the facial expression, the look in the eyes say 'Don't take this seriously, but . . .' This use of the body in sending signals of this kind is a matter which we shall take up again in some detail in the chapters to follow.

The function of the metacommunication or frame can be illustrated further by thinking of its use in a physical setting. The picture frame informs the viewer that the designs within the frame are to be treated differently from the designs on the surrounding wallpaper. A play on the paradox which is latent in the frame can be exploited by painting a picture with the same design as that of the wallpaper. Then, as long as the viewer realizes the difference, s/he experiences what the painter has done as a pleasing visual trick, a piece of surrealistic art. Note, however, that the picture frame does its job by telling us what to attend to and what to leave as background, while in itself remaining part of neither. The frame defines the picture as a painting – not a drawing on the wall – and does this by remaining unobtrusive.

It is easy therefore to use the idea of framing to show differences in the kinds of social situations in which people meet together. Knowing the frame tells the participants the kind of communications which are appropriate or to be expected. When attending the theatre, the audience knows that certain scenes will pass before it which are imaginary, are acted. In a psychotherapy group the participants know that things will be said which are personal and possibly upsetting but which are to be understood as 'part of the therapy'. The medical examination frames the actions of the doctor during the examination of a patient of the opposite sex, so that touches and presses are understood by both parties as aids to diagnosis, not expressions of personal feeling. However, to fix social episodes with labels of this kind is rather like designating some behaviour as 'play' and some as 'serious stuff', when we have seen that the essence of framing is that *any* behaviour can be framed and reframed. There are no pieces of 'play action' that appear only during play; rather, play consists of a transformation – a change – in the way that actions are carried out when done 'seriously'. Anything can be transformed into a joke, made to appear stupid, can be made a mockery of. This is consistent with what we have already said about appearances and the use of role distance in social behaviour, and means that social relationships cannot be divided up into the serious and the non-serious pieces. While playfulness as such may not permeate all of our exchanges, the use of frames or metacommunications almost certainly does.

The designation of a particular interaction as being wholly play or not-play is sometimes difficult to make, if not impossible. Take the following example. Two young sisters begin laughing and slapping at each other's arms. Their laughter and general demeanour make it clear to the onlooker that this is a game, and one that they have played before. As the slapping proceeds, however, it becomes progressively harder and the exchanges more deliberate, the laughter punctuated with howls when a blow strikes home. Eventually, one of the protagonists yells louder, turns away from the other and bursts into tears. There is now a complainant who cries 'Foul!' and a defendant who says it was all in fun. In effect, this is not play which turns at a specific moment into a combat, but all along was a game which posed the question, 'Is this play?' The ambiguity within the sisters' interaction allows for expressions of contest, of a little spite towards each other, and of pleasure at blows struck and avoided – all within the same exchange.

Extending this idea to other everyday relationships, it can be seen that wherever people joke, tease or lightly threaten there will be ambiguity about what is to be taken literally and what is to be taken metaphorically. When people say, 'Many a true word is spoken in jest', it is to this aspect of communication which they refer. For to think of playful exchanges as merely fanciful or unreal is to make a great mistake. Certain kinds of truths seem only approachable through 'play'; this is illustrated in the theatre and in the course of psychotherapy, where people talk *as if* things were different, or *as if* they were their father, or their spouse. Under the guise of play people are able to say things to each other which they would find difficult to express directly and coldly. Indeed, playfulness is the stuff of some of the claims which people make about themselves to others. A joke about someone's clothes, or about the situation which they share is often a good way to 'break the ice', and also to venture approaches which are not certain to succeed. Suggestions made with a laugh or a nudge are more easy to withdraw if the other person reacts badly to them. Then one can say, 'No, seriously though . .', and the proposition which *might* have been a joke or *might* have been a suggestion for real is taken out of the field of debate by its originator. A good example of this is flirting, in which things said with a sexual innuendo are thrown out to be deliberately ambiguous and, until the other person responds, hang in a limbo of uncertainty. 'Is this a joke or a proposition?' the other wonders. In effect, the response to the comment will help determine its status, so that what the first person claims s/he said (and even believes s/he said) may be crystallized only in the subsequent exchange, Of course, not every stage of an interaction will involve this sort of ambiguity. The point being made here is that this kind of playfulness is not exceptional but essential to people's working in and working out of their relationships with each other.

Framing and the reality of social life

Goffman (1975) took up Bateson's theory of play and used it to develop an account of how social life is framed in order to appear more or less real and serious. He introduced the term *keying* to indicate the way in which things done in a mundane way become transformed on such occasions. So a wave can be an expression of grief at parting, carried out in all seriousness, or else it can be done in a 'silly' or 'mocking' way to indicate fun and informality. The routine act of moving one's arm appears differently because it is keyed by the metacommunication of the person's demeanour and smiling face. The analogy of keying with musical keys is intentional; Goffman is pointing out that a change of key involves the same organization of notes (acts) but within a different frame. He used the simple example of a couple's kissing to note that this might be a 'husband' greeting his 'wife' or 'John' being careful with 'Mary's' make-up.

Goffman suggested that keying occurs on the basis of actions which form part of the everyday routines of life, which he called primary perspectives. In these realms, actions denote what they are 'normally' held to denote. So we might say to an enquirer, 'No, they aren't playing, they're really fighting'. One problem with this argument, from our point of view, is that how people come to judge what is 'really happening' cannot itself be taken out of the analysis. The argument gets complicated here, but Goffman himself recognized that some everyday keyed items will not be seen as such by many of us. For example, the kiss on the cheek or the slap on the back are *real* greetings, although the kiss is not sexual and the slap is not combative. The onlooker might well say, therefore, that these are everyday routines, whereas the student of social psychology would want to examine the ways in which they have been framed. For the purposes of this book, we must be content to say that there are actions which are not transformed when they are done 'really', 'actually' and 'literally'.

One of the main ways in which actions are transformed is through the key of make-believe. This covers what we have been calling playful behaviour, and is institutionalized in the media, most poignantly in the theatre. A play is a slice of life which is keyed in the production. Notice that, although the action of the play is 'just a story', the staging of the drama is real. This allows for the audience to be moved by the action on stage, and to laugh and to cry along with the players. The use of the key is one which the audience shares, so that someone might say, 'I thought the production was excellent, but what a tedious story.' Even then, make-believe has its limits, and Goffman notes that jokes are discredited where they breach the rules of bad taste, while film and theatre tread continually a thin line concerning what is 'art' and what is 'pornography'.

The theatre allows for the use of plays within plays, so transforming the 'fiction' of the main story into a 'fact' exploited by the sub-plot. Shakespeare used this device in different ways, including an occasion of explicit role-reversal in the play *I Henry IV*. The feckless young Prince Hal has spent much time debauching in the company of the fat and ageing Falstaff, and is to be brought to account for this by his father, King Henry. Anticipating that this is going to happen, Falstaff tells the prince:

FALSTAFF: Well, thou wilt be horribly chid tomorrow when thou comest to thy father: if thou love me, practise an answer.
PRINCE: Do thou stand for my father and examine me upon the particulars of my life.

Through this invitation, the two engage in a game of make-believe in which Falstaff plays the king, and the prince plays himself. However, within this playing Falstaff is keen to make a point to the future king about their relationship:

FALSTAFF [as King]: . . . And yet there is a virtuous man whom I have often noted in thy company, but I know not his name.
PRINCE: What manner of man, an it like your majesty?
FALSTAFF [as King]: A goodly portly man, i'faith and a corpulent; of a cheerful look, a pleasing eye and a most noble carriage; and, as I think, his age some fifty, or by'r lady, inclining to threescore; and now I remember me, his name is Falstaff . . .

There is much fun to be had in this pretence, as Falstaff continues:

FALSTAFF [as King]: . . . there is virtue in that Falstaff: him keep with, the rest banish.
And tell me now, thou naughty varlet, tell me, where hast thou been this month?
PRINCE: Dost thou speak like a king? Do thou stand for me, and I'll play my father.

In this exchange Falstaff uses the make-believe authority of the king to plead his own relationship with the man who will one day come to the throne. The unlikely nature of this plea tries the patience of the prince who suggests a better game, where they switch roles. During this the prince takes the opportunity, in his role as his father, to criticize himself and his companion in cutting terms:

PRINCE [as King]: Swearest thou, ungracious boy? henceforth ne'er look on me. Thou art violently carried away from grace: there is a devil haunts thee in the likeness of a fat old man; a tun of man is thy companion . . .

When Falstaff, playing the role of the prince, hears that the man in question is none other than himself, his role slips and he falls once more into special pleading:

FALSTAFF [as Prince]: . . . No, my good lord; banish Peto, banish Bardolph, banish Poins; but for sweet Jack Falstaff, kind Jack Falstaff, true Jack Falstaff, valiant Jack Falstaff, and therefore more valiant, being, as he is, old Jack Falstaff, banish not him thy Harry's company; banish plump Jack, and banish all the world.
PRINCE [as King]: I do, I will.

In this exchange Falstaff tries to defend himself (in his role as the prince) against the criticisms levelled against him, but in his desperation to save his reputation there is an increasing measure of reality in his play acting. This gradual closure of the distance between player and role communicates this urgency, which stands in contrast to the mock play acting when the two adopted complementary parts. The weakening of the framing of the role play is completed in the final words of the prince, in the role of his father the king, and of the king he is to become. 'I do, I will' seals Falstaff's fate. The significance of these words lies in the fact that they are spoken by the prince 'for real', so that with the collapse of the role play they rekey the action which is to follow.

This example illustrates that the framing and reframing of communications both changes the style of performance and the significance of what is to come. Ambiguity arises not only in the way that make-believe may allow two contradictory messages to be conveyed, but it can also place the past and the future of a relationship in question. When one partner mocks or deceives the other, this not only raises the question of how they will act in future, but it can also raise the question of whether the relationship was ever as good as was once believed. In the case of deep and long-term relationships, an answer to this question can be very elusive indeed.

On playfulness and the rules of behaviour

To conclude this chapter, we need to say something about the implications of play for understanding social interaction as governed by rules. On a superficial level, it might be thought that, where ceremonies such as weddings operate by means of rules, play does not do so. Like madness, play is unpredictable and irrational. From what we have seen so far of play-in-ritual, this would be a hasty conclusion to draw, and an erroneous one. Play does have rules, but so do rule-governed episodes involve imagination. The first claim, concerning play, is one that few social scientists would disagree with; the idea of finding a logic underlying what appears to be chaos has been of great appeal to them (Marsh, Rosser and Harré 1978). The theory of Harré and Secord attempts to show that all social episodes can be understood in terms of the rules which guide the actions of the participants. So we have rules for the dinner table, rules for holidaymaking, rules of the hairdressing salon, and so on. In a more detailed way it has been suggested that there are 'scripts' (borrowing again from the metaphor of the stage) by which people guide their actions, and know what kind of thing to say and to do (Schank and Abelson 1977). This, I would argue, presses the metaphor too far and flies in the face of what we know about playfulness as something which people induce in each other, not only do according to rules.

That there are rules in play seems indisputable, for otherwise it would be directionless and the players could not co-ordinate their actions. However, play has qualities which make it special; it preoccupies the participants and, as we have noted, it does not admit intrusions lightly. Play is pleasurable in itself, so that its end is in being played out; there is no short cut to play, nor is it easily undertaken in a deliberate manner (Winnicott 1971). When in Dickens's *Great Expectations* the young Pip is first taken to the house of the old recluse, Miss Haversham, she tells him:

> 'I sometimes have sick fancies,' she went on, 'and I have a sick fancy that I want to see some play. There, there!' with an impatient movement of the fingers of her right hand; 'play, play, play!'

Not surprisingly, the boy stands unable to carry out the command which, without the old lady's realizing it, cripples the implicit frame which the explicit message signifies.

The Russian psychologist Vygotsky (1976) noted the pleasurable basis to play, and remarked upon the fact that one cannot expect children to give an account of why or how they play. This does not mean that in play children are not conscious of what they are doing. On the contrary, Vygotsky claims that playing involves an awareness of things which, in real life, would go unnoticed. He cites the example of two sisters who play at being sisters (in effect playing at real life), for whom the important thing is to act out the role of sister with an awareness of the rules for doing this successfully. In this game they are aware of each other and of themselves in ways which they are not when acting normally. However, Vygotsky is not arguing that the rules must come first. Out of the routines of real life, transformed by the frame of play, is created a potential space for imaginary action, on the basis of which rules will emerge as the children play together. Equally important, Vygotsky argues that all rule-bound games require imagination. The pieces on the chess-board are not real queens, knights or bishops but stand for positions which they signify.

The communication in play of 'let's pretend' and in ritual of 'let us believe', which are ways of putting the frame into words, requires imagination. This means not only seeing the players and the pieces (e.g. chessmen) as symbols but each person's becoming preoccupied within the flow of action to which all contribute. Where in children's play imagination appears dominant and the rules have to be teased out, in adult play the rules are formalized and clear but the acts of imagination are hidden. However, all play and rituals involve people in rules and imaginings. We can extend this to say that all playful (or keyed) behaviour is both rule-governed and involves the imagination of those concerned. There is here another aspect of the ambiguity to which we have now frequently referred. Previously we have seen it in the person as performer/character, the social self as 'I'/'me', and in the group as it operates in terms of internal/external systems. To leave out one of these terms is to lose the essence of how people act ungraciously, with dignity or with style, each of which can be essential to the proper conduct of the occasion. Knowing the rules of a social occasion certainly helps students of social life to understand what is going on, but by itself it renders all the various things that people do together into a grey unity of 'rule-following'. Rules are made up, bent, broken and displayed to their better or their worse effect by the people who use them.

This study of playfulness and seriousness in social life undermines the covert assumption that relationships are just about decision making, predicting what the other person will do, or presenting oneself in the best possible light. Much work on play and ritual in social life remains to be done. However, it raises the issue of how these two styles of acting involve our bodily behaviour in distinct, yet similar ways. The discussion of how we use our bodies in social interaction is by now a substantial topic in social psychology and will be taken up in the two chapters to follow.

6

NON-VERBAL BEHAVIOUR AND COMMUNICATION

Studying face-to-face interaction presumes that people can see, hear and possibly touch each other. This is such a basic, taken-for-granted aspect of everyday life that it is perhaps not surprising that it was only in the 1960s that psychologists and sociologists began studying these things in earnest, under the label of non-verbal behaviour. (They were not the first to do so, however, because anthropologists studying various cultures had shown that people use their bodies in different ways as they go about their ordinary activities.) There has now developed a considerable body of research into non-verbal behaviour, and social scientists have examined in great.detail the regularities and the nuances of how people act as they speak. The implication that this knowledge is readily applied is a question which we shall discuss in the final chapter of the book, but it rests upon a further assumption which we shall examine in this chapter. It is this – there is a kind of universal code for understanding what people are feeling or wanting which can be read through their gestures and postures. This idea is at once intriguing and challenging, and not only for lay persons who would like to influence others or gain the upper hand in their social relationships. Social scientists, too, find this idea interesting because it holds out the possibility that there might be patterns in people's conduct which can be described and understood. It has provided the motivation for much of the work which I shall discuss in this chapter and has been the source of both illuminating ideas and some thorny problems as well.

When talking about how people form impressions of one another, the point was made that appearances depend upon both the expressiveness of one party and the interpretations of the other. In a literal sense, when you are speaking to other people they can see you (how you stand, how your facial expressions alter) in a way which is denied to you, the speaker. This is the issue of visibility, extended by Goffman into the proposition that what is seen by others includes what is, in a sense, given off by the speaker in ways which he or she does not intend. People do not just meet together in each others' physical presence but use their bodies to convey or endorse the culture of the group. It may be the laughter of friends at a party, or the quiet, respectful demeanour of mourners at a funeral, but the norms of group behaviour very definitely extend to the way that group members conduct themselves physically.

The discussion in chapter 4 showed that the body can be considered in terms of external characteristics which are differentially valued. These differences have implications for how the person might be welcomed into or progress within particular social groupings. Are you man or woman, tall or short, thin or fat, sound of wind and limb or handicapped – in sum, what sort of physical specimen are you? Although we might not wish it were so, there is evidence that we do judge each other (as strangers) in terms of attractiveness and grant to the more attractive the benefits of any social doubt (Berscheid and Walster 1974). The discussion of playfulness in chapter 5 turned upon the way in which the framing of episodes is often carried out by the use of the body. The sneer, the shrug, the hand on the knee, each in its own way says something about the relationship which is being invoked or invited. We can see from these examples, drawn out within this brief résumé, that our social relationships are not mental events, floating in some psychological ether, but are grounded in our physical being. Of course, we are able to interact with people who are not in our presence (the simple example of the telephone conversation tells us that); and we can form social bonds with people whom we can never meet (a political prisoner in another country, for example). However, for the purposes of understanding how people relate to one another in the course of everyday life, we first need to examine how social scientists have studied the question of communicating with the body.

What is meant by non-verbal behaviour?

As we shall see in this chapter, the field of non-verbal behaviour is not as easily defined as one might at first expect. In particular, the question of whether gestures are actual communications or merely behaviours is a key issue, and one which will take up much of our attention. For the moment I will use the term *non-verbal behaviour* to cover the topic at hand, although later on I shall want to point out the importance of choosing our terminology more carefully. In spite of these cautions, it is possible to make some broad distinctions which will help us to decide which kinds of behaviours are usually covered by the term 'non-verbal'. First, we can distinguish between those things which people say using language and those that they do outside language; this is a distinction between verbal and non-*verbal* aspects of experience. Second, there is a distinction to be made between communications made by the use of our vocal organs and those made by means of other parts of the body. We can term this the *vocal* versus the *non-vocal* difference (Laver and Hutcheson 1972). If we put these two distinctions together, the table below can be obtained. The usefulness of this table is to show us that the superficial difference between 'saying and doing' is inadequate for the purpose of understanding what happens when we communicate with our bodies.

	VOCAL	NON-VOCAL
Verbal	Speech	Sign language
Non-verbal	Intonation	Gestures

The verbal/vocal condition is speech as we normally think of it: people using words to communicate with each other. The essence of words is that they are part of a language, a shared system of symbols for representing objects and ideas. When social scientists speak of words as symbols they are drawing attention to this sharing of language, essential because there are no pregiven attachments of words to the objects (or ideas) which they represent. In English the word for 'man's best friend' is 'dog'; in French it is 'chien'; in German it is 'Hund'. This is often referred to as the *arbitrary* relation of words to the objects which they represent and is one of the ways in which language differs from other communications. I mention this now because we shall see that one of the issues in the explanation of bodily communication is the degree to which it can or should be considered as being 'like language'.

Language need not be communicated with the vocal organs. People who are deaf and/or dumb have the mental capacity, of course, to use language, to think and to express themselves in terms of arbitrary symbols. Sign language is the form of communication which uses non-vocal means to convey verbal symbols, so that we should not confuse this with the gestures which other people make in the course of everyday speech. It also alerts us to the possibility that individuals who, for some reason, either cannot or choose not to use their voices can nevertheless communicate linguistically in other ways, by means of Morse code, for example, or by semaphore.

The realm of non-verbal behaviour as it is generally understood is defined by the non-verbal and the non-vocal category in the table above. This includes all things done outside language except with the vocal organs. This exception defines the category of non-verbal communications which accompany words (the vocal dimension) in the act of speaking them. Let us just dispense with this condition first before returning to the field of gesture proper. When we speak, we use our voices in ways which are common to the group and also peculiar to what we are saying at the time. This condition, therefore, includes people's accents and also the intonation which they give to the words as they say them (e.g. pitch and loudness of voice, drawl of words). What is special about these non-verbal signals is that they are inevitable accompaniments to the act of speaking. This does not mean, however, that they can't be used without saying words. To say 'Mmm?' to somebody is to intone in a way which uses these abilities without actually saying any words.

The field of gesture proper can be considered to be the use of the body to communicate outside or alongside spoken language. An example of the first might be the way that someone avoids the glance of another person or takes the arm of someone to draw them into a confidence (these are called *extra*linguistic communications because they are carried out independently of speech). Examples of the second kind include expressive gestures, with hands and face particularly, which accompany the words which people say to one another. These gestures are called *para*linguistic communications because they depend upon the verbal context for their meaning; they also 'shape' the form of the message which is given in the words. The distinction being drawn here is between gestures which can somehow be tied to spoken language and gestures which are free of what people are saying at the time. So, a wolf whistle is not paralanguage because it stands on its own in achieving its end. A widening of the eyes and expansive movement of the fingers, however, might mean nothing in itself but, coupled with the statement that '. . . what will happen when this story blows . . .', the listener gains an impression of an impending furore. Paralanguage, therefore, must be defined always in terms of what the person is saying; to the extent that a gesture can be understood on its own or occurs without meaning in the absence of spoken language (e.g. an eyebrow twitch), then it can be considered as extralinguistic activity (Abercrombie 1968).

This particular categorization of non-verbal behaviour is useful as a starting point, but it should not be taken by the reader to be a cast-iron definition of the topic of non-verbal behaviour. In fact, although it helps to define the field of study, it also raises problems as a result. This can be understood partly as a consequence of certain behaviours falling into more than one category. The eyebrow twitch mentioned above may be an extralinguistic gesture, signifying nothing, or it may be an accompaniment to the words of the speaker. It becomes unsatisfactory to try to allocate particular gestures to the different conditions once one realizes that their membership is dependent upon the situation in which they take place.

At this stage in the argument, is it then possible to say something definite about the relationship between words and gestures? The view of gesture as paralanguage would appear to make non-verbal behaviours dependent upon speech, in that the things people do with their hands and faces will be amplifying, modulating or otherwise accompanying the meaning which the words set out. An alternative argument has been made, however, which places the emphasis differently. From this position (which is similar in many respects to the framing argument given in chapter 5) non-verbal behaviour sets the context within which speech is delivered and heard (Watzlawick, Beavin and Jackson 1967). This means that the wink of the eye or the raised eyebrow are not so much accompaniments to the words spoken but are signs made by the speaker to initiate a framework or context which will tell how the words to follow should be taken. Clearly these are two different balances of verbal and non-verbal communications, and it is not possible within the simple scheme introduced above to say anything about how and under what conditions these might alter.

In a broad sense, the issue of the way that verbal and non-verbal signals affect each other can be resolved into the question of which will be the most important in contributing to the impression gained of the speaker. Social psychologists have carried out experiments to examine this problem, asking subjects to make judgements about a message with varying verbal and non-verbal components. In this way a person can be presented with a positive message said in a negative manner, or a negative message said in a positive manner. Results of some studies have shown that non-verbal communications carry more weight (Argyle, Salter, Nicholson, Williams and Burgess 1970), though one experiment indicated that what people rated most negatively was the discrepancy itself, i.e. they mistrusted all messages in which verbal and non-verbal signals were contradictory (Bugental, Kaswan and Love 1970). (This is what one would expect from Goffman's claim that an effective impression resides in the consistency of the message given with information given off.) The effect of the discrepancy was especially marked for children who perhaps did not understand some messages as 'jokes' which adults would perceive. These results suggest that the importance of verbal as compared with non-verbal signals is not likely to be a static condition but will change according to the situation and to the people concerned.

One consequence of considering non-verbal behaviour in relation to language only is that it became primarily a study of how bodily communication aids, helps to convey or otherwise signals things about talk (Beattie 1983). This approach has meant that the field has been defined, literally, as (non)verbal communication, so that it was set out from the perspective of theorists interested in the use of language. The very title shows that it was a topic which was defined by default, meaning that it contained those aspects of behaviour which, though not speech, came to matter only because they made a difference to speech and to how it was interpreted. Some of the problems which follow from this will be discussed in the sections to follow, while the advantages of taking a wider view will be presented in chapter 7.

Approaches to the study of non-verbal behaviour

Without doing too great an injustice to the wide range of work into bodily communication, one can divide the topic according to two main approaches taken to its study. One is the *structural approach*, which focuses upon bodily gestures as if they formed a communication system (Birdwhistell 1971; Scheflen 1972, 1979). From this perspective head nods, sighs, hand movements and facial expressions are not to be taken as separate indicators of inner feelings or vehicles for carrying independent meanings. Instead, they are made in relation to one another, so that their meaning lies in the patterned way in which they occur together.

We can use an example to show one form of this approach (Watzlawick, et al. 1967). At breakfast time, a husband is concerned only to read his newspaper; his wife, on the other hand, wants them to talk together. When the wife talks, the husband makes a brief reply and pulls the newspaper up higher to block his wife's view of his face. She, in her turn, presses on with her conversation, as part of which she remonstrates with her husband for not talking to her at breakfast time. In reply he insists that she stop 'nagging' at him and let him get on with reading his paper. If we could ask each of them in turn why they act as they do, we might find that the husband's explanation is that the only defence he has against his wife's nagging at him is to bury himself in his paper; if 'she didn't go on so much' he might not have to do it. The wife's explanation is that she only 'goes on' at her husband because he 'won't say a word to me at breakfast'. Each of them has an explanation from their own particular position which accounts for their 'reasonable' behaviour in terms of the 'unreasonable' attitudes of the other.

Instead of looking at the behaviour of the husband and wife separately, we can see it as a patterned sequence of moves (as in a game), in which husband-withdrawal follows wife-nagging which follows husband-withdrawal which in turn follows wife-nagging and so on. The meaning of each of the behaviours is to be understood, not in terms of the separate attitudes of the two people concerned, but in terms of the pattern to which the parts contribute and which, in turn, sustains them. This is rather like the idea of the notes which go to make up a melody, where the tune (the 'music' made by husband and wife together) is constructed by the separate notes but gives to each one an aesthetic feel because of its place in the whole. We have already met the idea that what is important in social action is the way that acts are put together, the key or frame which lends a different colour to what is done even though the acts retain their relationship to one another. The structural approach to bodily communication is similar in looking always at the pattern of the whole exchange in order to understand what is taking place. Instead of making the comparison with music, one can make the more usual analogy with language. The meaning conveyed depends upon the words selected from among the set possible and upon the way in which they are put together. A particular word's meaning is discovered not in itself – as if there was an absolute correspondence between the word and what it signifies – but in the context of its use. Part of this context is given by the other words surrounding it, and part by the situation in which they are read or spoken. One strand of the structuralist approach to bodily communication has been the attempt to treat bodily gesture as if it had just this sort of grammar to it, a non-verbal but none the less language-like system with a code which can be understood.

I shall pick up some of the issues raised by the structuralist approach in a moment, because they are central to the question of whether bodily conduct can be treated as a communication system. At this point we need to describe the other main approach to studying non-verbal behaviour which has been called the *external variable* (sometimes 'psychological') perspective (Duncan 1969). The title comes from the range of studies carried out by psychologists using the experimental method to relate particular gestures or postures to other (external) variables in which they are interested. For example, one might want to discover whether there are differences between the sexes in a certain behaviour, such as ways of holding one's body while talking. Other questions might relate to the effect of obscuring or hindering the use of a particular way of communicating, such as eye contact or facial expression. In all of these cases the interest is in the *function* of bodily conduct; what does it do, how does it work, what does it convey? The concept of function indicates that, for many psychologists, non-verbal behaviour is not treated as a whole system to be examined and charted but as a collection of relatively discrete 'channels' through which messages are conveyed and upon which verbal exchanges are balanced. The main difference between the two approaches lies, therefore, in the focus of interest. For the structuralists (or, as some called themselves, 'behavioural systems' theorists) the problem of bodily conduct is one of describing the communication system of which gestures are a part; for the psychologists, non-verbal behaviour is not so much a problem as another field in which to address such questions as how interactions are organized and social status differences maintained.

There is a third approach which needs to be mentioned, although this will take up little space in this book. It is the *ethological* approach, drawn from and sometimes practised by scientists who also study animal behaviour (Hinde 1972). There is a long tradition, going back to Charles Darwin, of seeing animal (and therefore human) behaviour as being essentially adaptive. This means that expressive behaviour, from snarls to raising one's eyebrows, can be interpreted in terms of the evolutionary background of the species. At the back of this reasoning lie some assumptions which some social scientists find hard to accept. In particular, comparisons of humans with animals in terms of apparent emotions (aggression, fear, love) assume that these words mean (even roughly) the same thing when applied across the different species. As part of this assumption, there is assumed to be some fixed correspondence between the behaviour and the feeling being expressed. We have already seen that this kind of absolutist correspondence between action and feeling cannot be assumed. If it did exist, then there would be little problem about discovering the non-verbal code, for it would already be public property. While there is no doubt that we, as human beings, are constrained by our bodies to be able to do only certain things (our muscles allow some things, forbid others), the idea that our bodily conduct is somehow 'closer to nature' is arguably a fallacy which hinders rather than helps our understanding of these problems.

Some categories of gesture in communication

In this section I want to provide an overview of how gestures have been understood as part of everyday communication. For simplicity's sake, these behaviours are those defined within the scheme given earlier as being non-vocal/non-verbal. The organization of the discussion will follow the lines laid down by Ekman and Friesen (1969a), two investigators whose researches have overlapped the structural and the psychological approaches to the topic (see also Ekman 1977). Their understanding of gesture is itself based upon one of the earliest attempts to study this problem in a systematic way. About the time of the start of the Second World War, an Argentinian anthropologist working in the USA studied the differences in conversational gestures of immigrant Jews and Italians in New York (Efron 1972). Efron's work was carried out in the context of the claims made by Nazi writers in Germany that personality (and, hence, gesture) is racially determined. He was able to show that this is not true; that, while there are cultural differences in the way that people use their bodies while communicating, these are subject to change. Second-generation Jewish and Italian immigrants to the USA were more like native Americans in their gestures than were their parents who had originally come from Europe. In the course of making this study, Efron had devised a classification of gestures according to their function in relation to speech and to the individuals' relationships in general. Two of these have been developed by Ekman and Friesen, the *emblem* and the *illustrator*. Together with a third, the *body manipulator*, they provide a scheme for describing how people use gesture as they converse.

Emblems are actions which have a specific verbal meaning, known either to most members of the culture or to those in particular sub-cultures or groups. Included in this category are 'V-signs', the 'thumbs-up' signal and the wave of greeting. These gestures stand out as having, as it were, an existence of their own, because they have an agreed-upon meaning within the community. They have a symbolic feature to them, something which, it was said earlier, is a special characteristic of language. The reason for this is that emblems stand for something, in an agreed way, like a shorthand communication. They might be arbitrary too, having no commonly known relationship to what they signify (e.g. the V-sign). Others are not arbitrary but contain in the action some essential element of what it is to which they refer (e.g. the arm action which says, 'Come over here,' or the hand cupped behind the ear which says, 'Speak up, I can't hear you!'). This latter kind of relationship is known as *iconic*, the act being in some way an 'icon' or part representation of what it signifies.

Emblems make up the group of gestures of which it is easiest to think of examples (the fist shaken at someone, the finger to the lips directed at the person with the loud voice). The reason for this has already in part been given, that they communicate a relatively specific meaning. Also emblems are acts for which we often have a verbal label or can imitate them readily if asked to do so. In short, they are gestures of which people can be readily conscious. This does not mean that they always have to be carried out consciously: people may make a fist in the course of a conversation and not realize that they have done so. Nor do emblems have to be recognized by all for what they are. Across different groups within a culture certain gestures may carry little meaning at all. Also, emblematic communication can be improvised if necessary where spoken communication is made difficult or impossible; the game of Charades demands precisely this ability. Indeed, the use of these forms of gesture is often found on such occasions, although, along with other forms of bodily communication, they should not be thought of as a mere substitute for speech.

Illustrators are gestures which are closely tied to speech. In that sense the term includes much that was referred to earlier on as 'paralanguage'. Ekman and Friesen used Efron's (1972) classification of different kinds of illustrators, such as the *baton*, the finger or hand which 'beats the tempo of mental locomotion'. Other gestures are easy to recognize, such as the stabbing finger, the waving arm or the pounding fist, all of which emphasize the meaning of the words as they are spoken. The degree to which people use their hands and arms while talking depends upon their culture and upon their individual inclination. The use of illustrators in speaking is something which is learned in the course of our upbringing and is open to relearning, when we are more likely to be aware of what we are doing. Efron found that, among his Italian subjects, these gestures had a declamatory function, being used by one individual at a time in order to make his or her point. Among his Jewish subjects, however, illustrators were used by both speakers at the same time, almost in a competitive duologue. Indeed, he remarks upon the traditional Jewish ploy of holding the other person's arm so that he or she cannot gesticulate. To people of a culture used to communicating with illustrators, this is almost synonymous with having someone prevent you speaking altogether!

When do people use illustrators? Ekman and Friesen suggest that this happens when we cannot find a word, so that perhaps we snap our fingers or make a circling movement with our hands. More obvious is the change in gesture which accompanies and also signifies a change in mood. When people are very enthusiastic, they may gesticulate more as their words fail to convey the feeling which they are trying to get across. As well as this, we are used to seeing speech punctuated with abrupt use of the hands and arms when people are angry. The essential characteristic of all illustrative gesture is that it does not stand alone but is employed in the context of speech. Note that we are not here logging which movements are emblems and which ones are illustrators. Sometimes the same movement can be used for either, as when a man describes an attractive woman by tracing an hourglass shape in the air with his fingers. Ekman (1977) used this example to argue that we can only call this an emblem if we know that it is a sign shared by the culture of which the man is a member. Clearly the use of the body as a vehicle of communication depends upon the meanings which are placed upon it by the community as a whole and, as we shall see, the degree to which the culture accepts gestures as legitimate forms of communication.

The third class of behaviours which Ekman and Friesen describe are body manipulators. These are different to the previous two classes of gesture in that they involve one part of the body's doing something to another part. More important still, these actions are seen by those observing the person not to have been carried out with the explicit intention of communicating anything. Examples of body manipulators include scratching one's head, fiddling with a shoe lace, biting one's lower lip or covering the eyes with one's hands in the course of speaking. Although these movements tend to be unintended (we are often unaware of doing them, unless someone draws our attention to them), this does not mean that they are seen to be of little importance. To see other people begin to wriggle in their seat, scratch the side of their nose repeatedly or pull at a loose thread on their jacket might indicate to us that they are no longer attending to what we are saying. Indeed, this class of behaviours has provided the evidence from which psychoanalysts and others interested in people's problems have drawn inferences about personality. While body manipulators are different from emblems in being unintended, they are distinct from illustrators in having little relation to the flow or structure of the interaction. Fiddling with a shoelace might well continue as first one person speaks and then the other; rubbing one's nose is not connected with a change of topic in the conversation. The inclusion of this class of behaviours, in spite of these differences, shows that they can be of importance in affecting the way in which people relate to one another. There are two reasons for this which we shall consider briefly below.

The first reason is that these apparently involuntary body movements tell us something about the other person: is she listening? is she nervous? is she telling the truth? Ekman and Friesen (1969b) have argued that various parts of the body are differently equipped to send messages about the people concerned or about the meeting itself. The face, both in its anatomical construction and because it is a visible focus, is quick at sending messages and at covering up 'leaks' of information. The need to be consistent in one's presentation – to keep a straight face – is the point emphasized by Goffman in his argument that the selves which individuals put forward are subject to checking by others. This means that we scan each other's face while talking, monitoring the constant, often fleeting, expressions against our understanding of each other at the time. Because clues given off by the face are often transitory and are quickly covered up, Ekman and Friesen state that it is not as good a guide to leakages as the hands or the legs and feet. Indeed, because the legs and feet are often less visible, and because they play a relatively minor role in intended bodily expression, they are less subject to voluntary control. This means that leg and foot movements are potentially better sources of information for checking by the attentive observer than are other parts of the body.

The second reason why body manipulators are worth studying is that they are not only used as clues about individuals but reflect something about the interaction itself. Goffman (1971) proposed that 'impression management' demands that people control the way that they use their bodies in this way. It is not good manners to pick one's nose or to scratch one's crotch in the company of other people. The more formal the situation the greater the limit on the acceptability of such behaviours. When, after a period of intense or formal discussion, people complete their business, it is not unusual to see them carrying out just these sort of actions, stretching, rubbing their eyes, or moving around on their chairs. While, as mentioned above, particular body manipulators are not related to the flow of interaction, we should not overlook the fact that these behaviours are also subject to social control. (We shall look at just this issue in more detail in the chapter to follow.)

What are we to make of the three classes of non-verbal behaviour given above? They do not provide an exhaustive list of all of the different kinds of non-verbal behaviours but indicate some of the issues which we shall need to take up if we are to get nearer to some kind of theory of bodily communication. As I have already pointed out, the mere listing of details of non-verbal communications does not get us very far in understanding how these fit into a psychology of appearances and social groups. Note that particular body movements cannot be allocated to specific categories with any certainty that they belong there and nowhere else. You can point your finger at someone in the course of making a point in a conversation (an illustrator) or as an emblem for saying 'I mean you.' Similarly, you can rub your nose as a sign to another person (an emblem), or in the course of listening to what they say (a body manipulator). The exact status of the movement depends upon the context of the action and upon the intentions of the people concerned. These might be studied by an industrious and particular social scientist, but still they might not provide the information needed for us to set down each body movement in the classification with confidence. Why? Because the people concerned might not agree as to what each one intended, and to the interpretations to be made of the bodily actions which did occur. Many arguments begin not with a dispute over the content of what will be the disagreement, but with claim and counter-claim as to whether a voice was raised or whether one of the people concerned did or did not make a particular expression. From this we can see that we have a point of contact with our earlier discussion on appearances and expressions.

Is it necessary that people are aware of their non-verbal behaviour? From what has been said already, it is clear that this is not the case. Social psychologists, in particular, have studied the function of a whole range of subtle behaviours such as eye contact, touch and distance between people to show that these make differences to relationships without our being either aware of them or being able to say how we do them (Argyle 1969). These behaviours are sometimes called *regulators* and operate not just to modify particular words or phrases, but to control the flow of the whole exchange itself. Once broadened in this way, non-verbal behaviour ceases to be easily thought of as a kind of code supplementary to language. Indeed, the identification of non-verbal behaviour with non-verbal communication and with bodily conduct begins to look distinctly fragile. All three terms seem to say much the same thing when we have emblems or illustrators (e.g. facial expressions, hand movements) in the backs of our minds as the ideal or most common gestures. However, once we accept that only some behaviours are intended, only some come within the awareness of all the people involved, and some are the subject of different interpretations by those individuals, then we see that these terms are perhaps not interchangeable. Just as the behaviours are not easily classified, so the terms in which we make the classification need to be kept under review.

Emotion and the universality of non-verbal behaviour

Efron's study of the gestural styles of Jewish and Italian immigrants showed two things. First, that gesture is partly specific to particular cultures and, second, that it is subject to change. These findings bear upon the question of whether there are any universals in non-verbal behaviour, i.e. are there any non-verbal behaviours which mean the same all over the world? (This is an ongoing debate. See Bull 1983; Eibl-Eibesfeldt 1979.) Efron's work suggests that there are likely to be differences between cultures, something that the anthropologists had noted from their field studies. Examining not only facial expressions but the way in which people use their whole body in everyday life, descriptions like the following were made, this one about the people of Bali:

> The more co-ordinated and disciplined the motion of the body becomes, the smaller the muscle groups with which a Balinese operates. Where an American or a New Guinea native will involve almost every muscle in his body to pick up a pin, the Balinese merely uses the muscles immediately relevant to the act, leaving the rest of the body undisturbed.
>
> (Mead 1942)

The different ways of life of people in various cultures might lead us to think that there would be little in the way of shared gestures, but the common condition of people who must inhabit the same body form suggests that certain 'basic expressions' might apply to all. (The inverted commas are meant to show that the status of these expressions as basic is a matter of contention.) Among these are emotional expressions, such as anger, hate, pleasure or pain, which it is assumed we read directly from the face and demeanour of other people. There has been a tendency to treat emotional behaviours as somewhat different from other forms of bodily conduct, accepting that they sometimes occur in response to conditions rather than as part of the give and take of social interaction. This is a somewhat limited approach, however, as we shall see from a consideration of studies examining emotional expressions in different cultures.

One study investigated the perceptions of members of a New Guinea tribe who had had little or no contact with people from other cultures (Ekman and Friesen 1971). They were asked to match pictures showing different facial expressions to stories telling of someone feeling a particular emotion. In this case the stories related to the life of the tribespeople, while the pictures were of Westerners posing one of six emotions – happiness, sadness, anger, fear, disgust or surprise. It was found that the New Guinea subjects could match pictures to stories and did so to an equal degree whether they had some or no experience of outsiders. (Evidence from work with babies suggests that there may be some built-in readiness to discriminate between certain facial expressions, although this does not mean that there is a universal code for understanding expressive behaviour (Bull 1983).) However, focusing upon a photograph of a posed facial expression is simply not representative of the range and the variety of expressive behaviours in which people engage, nor does it allow for the ways in which these 'basic' emotions are transformed in the course of lives lived in different cultures. As children grow up they learn, according to the cultural norms, how much emotional expression they are allowed to engage in, and which specific behaviours are tolerated or expected by their elders (Geertz 1959).

Nevertheless, there is a difficulty about teasing out the cultural from the biological components in emotional expression. Even where we see the mourners at funerals in two cultures making different facial expressions, we cannot be certain that 'grief is culture-specific' because we don't know that death means the same to the two peoples concerned (Ekman 1977). Even if there is a common emotion, the norms which say how one should behave, how one should (or should not) show one's feelings, will intervene. In a study using Japanese and American subjects who saw a disturbing film, there was no difference in the reactions of the two groups when watching as individuals (Ekman and Friesen 1971). When seated with a colleague of the experimenters, however, the Japanese subjects restrained their emotional reactions, looking polite and smiling more. Ekman and Friesen explain this as being due to the display rules which apply in Japanese society concerning the public show of one's emotions. These display rules are not, of course, limited to Japan: all cultures have norms about what it is appropriate to feel (i.e. to admit, either verbally or bodily) in particular situations. They will vary for people of different ages (children's displays are tolerated – for a time), and of different experience. New sailors who are seasick and medical students who faint in theatre are gently chided and learn to mask their feelings with other behaviours.

The concept of display rule, in its turn, makes it difficult to see how cross-cultural studies can ever bracket out the societal expectations which would allow 'real emotion' to be shown. There can be no certainty that, when people look at a photograph of a face showing 'disgust', it is seen as something 'basic' rather than as a picture of a person obeying the expectations of his or her culture. The attempt to tie down bodily expression to particular emotions rests upon the assumption that such feelings have some biological existence. It is beyond the scope of this book to take this question further, but it is sufficient for our purposes to note that this can tell us nothing about the broader range of bodily conduct in which we are interested. Specifically, it cannot explain the actions which are carried out, not in passion or as a reaction to events, but with feeling, to produce in others the impression of dignity, of contempt, of disdain or of beauty.

Behaviour, communication and the question of a code

So far in this chapter I have discussed non-verbal behaviour as if it were a communication system. As pointed out earlier, this is the approach that has been traditionally taken to the topic, either seeking to describe in ever greater detail the specific movements which make up the system (structuralist approach) or else relating particular behaviours to differences in the situation (psychological approach). Behind both of these lie certain assumptions, strengthened in each case by the choice of conversation as either the typical setting in which to study bodily communication, or else as the model of what a communication system should be. It was perhaps inevitable, therefore, that by pressing the comparison with verbal communication, researchers into non-verbal behaviour would eventually be criticized for failing to establish the common properties of language and gesture which they had claimed all along.

The critique came in a paper which challenged the claim that social scientists were providing accounts of non-verbal behaviour as a communication system (Wiener, Devoe, Rubinow and Geller 1972). These authors based their criticisms upon a number of points which we shall examine in turn. First among these was that experimenters had paid insufficient attention to the way that gestures *are made*, being primarily concerned with the ways in which they *are interpreted*. Indeed, the form of many studies was (and continues to be) one in which subjects are asked to make judgements about some aspect of non-verbal behaviour. This places the emphasis upon the observer whose interpretations give significance to the actions being studied. As a consequence, any piece of behaviour might be deemed suitable for investigation as 'non-verbal behaviour', so that subjects could make inferences on the basis of posture, or hand movements, or facial expression or even head scratching. The problem with this line of inquiry is that the choice of behaviour to be studied is arbitrary; anything can be studied on the assumption that it might be 'communication'. Put bluntly, this means that, if a body movement can be seen, it can be interpreted; and, if it can be interpreted, it surely must mean that the person in question is communicating.

Wiener *et al.* disputed this assumption and said that such experimenters were fusing the idea of a sign with the concept of communication. While a body movement may be taken as a sign of something, say nervousness or fatigue, this is not the same as saying that the person is communicating fatigue or nervousness by means of these movements. They compared this situation to someone seeing the approach of dark heavy clouds and inferring, not just that rain is imminent, but that the clouds are communicating, via a code involving darkness and heaviness, that it will soon rain. Using this example they argued that a sign (of rain, of nervousness) implies only that an observer has made an inference, whereas communication requires two further conditions. First, the person behaving must do so with the intention of making something public; second, there must be a socially shared code for enabling this to be done. These two conditions hold for spoken language, at least in principle. When people speak they know they do so, and to what point; also, the use of language is only possible because people share the conventional word usage, and the way in which words are put together.

Let us take up the issue of whether behaviour needs to be intended for it to be communication, using examples to help us do this. I once heard a lady talk of the change in people's reactions to her following an operation to her face which left her with an upward turn to one corner of her mouth. As a consequence she was perceived by people as smiling at them, and this prompted them to smile at her in return. Clearly, in this case, the surgically produced smile was informative rather than intentional and was taken by others as being the latter when it was not. As an exercise, the reader can make a listing of those things which he or she thinks of as being informative or intentional. Certain actions might easily be entered on one side, say waving to someone to join you, while others clearly belong on the other – eyeblinks and posture included. One does not have to pursue this exercise for very long, however, without realizing that several of one's entries might appear in either category, depending on the situation. Sometimes one corrects or modifies one's posture deliberately (e.g. the protruding stomach, the drooping shoulders), but at other times we are unaware of the posture which we adopt and it is there for others to interpret as they will. More important, however, is the fact that the definition of a piece of 'non-verbal behaviour' depends upon the standpoint of the person making it.

From the position of the actor, a gesture may be intentional and designed to communicate a point. The other people observing, however, might miss the intent, crediting it as being something which was simply given off by the person and therefore open to their interpretation. For example, when someone sighs deeply at a comment made by another person, and the latter asks 'Are you tired?', the sigh is for one of them a pointed communication about the conversation and, for the other person, information about the listener's bodily state. Of course, it could just as easily be the other way round. The person sighs involuntarily, but the speaker quickly responds with, 'Am I boring you?' Now the status of the sigh as information or as communication is reversed between the two individuals. Take this one stage further. When challenged in this way the person who made the sigh might say, 'No, no, of course not, I'm really interested.' The speaker might be satisfied, in which case the sigh is consigned to the 'informational' category. And yet – the person who sighed thinks, 'Well, perhaps I am tired, and this is beginning to get a little boring . . .', and before long he sighs again.

The purpose of this example is to show that the allocation of particular acts to the categories of 'informational' or 'intentional' cannot be done in an *a priori* way. It depends upon the accounts which both actor and observer might give of the behaviour in question. This is complicated by the fact that people do not divide their actions between these categories in everyday experience. By this I mean that many things that we do are *part* of our performance and no more; they are intended as such, but not to be taken in isolation and examined. This is common to many people's experience, becoming sometimes the source of irritation and the point of dispute. In the course of a heated discussion you bang your fist on the table to make a point. The other person takes exception to this and says that there is no point in trying to bully him. The point at issue is whether the banged fist was a communication (designed by you to coerce) or a matter of information, part of your manner of delivery. In truth, it can be both, for it would be untrue to say that the banged fist was unintended; you meant to speak strongly, as part of which and in the course of speaking, you banged your fist on the table. However, exactly how the fist would resound on the wood was not part of your prediction, and indeed from what we have seen when discussing the ideas of G.H. Mead, need not be so.

From this illustration one can see that the question of intention, of how non-verbal behaviour becomes communication, should not be reduced to a matter of what the actor, alone, had in mind at the time. This notion might hold for specific gestures, such as V-signs or winks of the eye, but it simply does not hold for the way in which people conduct their whole bodies. I make this comparison in order to point up the difference between a study of specific 'channels' of communication (e.g. eye contact, posture, hand movement) and a study of the body taken as a whole. It would seem that a ready division of non-verbal behaviour into informational and communicative rests upon the former. If, as was once said, we 'speak with our vocal organs but converse with our entire bodies' (Abercrombie 1968), then restricting the study of non-verbal behaviour to specific channels first abstracts and then artificially distorts their use as vehicles of communication.

Let us now consider the second criticism of Wiener *et al.*'s, that non-verbal behaviour researchers must come up with a code shared by the society or group under study. If there is a 'body language' to examine, then it should have units of behaviour (like words), each with its own specific significance, so that one could see how the separate actions are put together using something like the rules of grammar. They argue that this has not been demonstrated. Instead, we have the results of studies which show that in given situations people's actions are interpreted in certain ways. The question then is, are these non-verbal behaviours not so much communications about something, but rather signs *of* something, of which they are a part? When a subordinate stands in front of the desk at which his or her boss is seated, are these people communicating status or are they, in their bodily dispositions, reflecting it? The two conditions are not the same and must not be confused. Using the Wiener argument, we should need to show the other thing which is being indicated by the people's postures (i.e. what they signify). To say that this is 'their different status in the firm' is to go around in a circle, for this is what defines their relationship *for them* in the first place. We, of course, as imaginary onlookers, might have inferred the status difference from peeking in at the door. However, from what has been said already about informational evidence, it is clear that we must not project our interpretation ('A is the boss; B is the subordinate') into the intentions of the two people concerned.

How should we summarize this critical overview? The first and most obvious point is that we should not equate non-verbal behaviour with non-verbal communication. All bodily conduct is not communicative, in the sense that it is used to convey messages, or even to support conversation. For researchers interested in the traditional problems the task becomes one of defining more precisely how parts of the body are used in the course of speech. The implications of the critique are wider than this, however. For if bodily action as a whole is not best thought of as a language-like communication system, then how should it be thought of? What lies behind the veil of that all too comfortable term, 'non-verbal'?

A new view of expressive behaviour

The new view of bodily expression which I want to introduce here actually antedates the experimental research about non-verbal communication. It is new to psychology, although developed by the philosopher Susanne Langer (1957) from detailed study in the field of aesthetics. Langer's concern was to understand artistic expression, such as that conveyed by music, dance or the plastic arts. She was particularly critical of attempts to explain these things as the outward expression of the artist's personal emotions, a view which fails to explain the felt significance of performances of dance or music. Instead, Langer argued that music, for example, is a formulation or representation of moods and ideas which has its own logical form. Listening to an orchestral work is not an exercise in recapturing what, for example, Mozart felt as he composed it, but experiencing through its form the subtle complexes of feeling attributable to human beings. It was Mozart's ability to articulate, in musical form, his knowledge or experience of life that makes this communication possible. Langer's point is that artistic expression has a logic, and that its strength lies in the fact that it 'articulates forms which language cannot set forth'. The crux of her argument is that music and dance reveal a different way of communicating about things from language; like words, artistic expressions make things conceivable (e.g. tragedy, remorse) but unlike words the means of articulation are presentational, not discursive.

This is a notion which does not slip easily into an introductory text on social interaction. Yet the point Langer makes has been touched upon by social scientists too. Bateson (1987), whose ideas on framing were discussed in chapter 5, has quoted the dancer Isadora Duncan as once saying: 'If I could tell you what it meant, there would be no point in dancing it.' He interprets this to mean, not that 'it' would be better said in words if this were possible, but that dance communicates something whose form is lost once it is put into words. Music and dance can set out what we clumsily call feelings in ways which words simply cannot do, but these presentational and dramatic forms are poor substitutes for words when it comes to analytic thinking. The syntax (grammar) of language is strong compared to that of artistic forms; by comparison the semantics (meaning) of art is strong as compared to that of language. Lest this last point be misunderstood, what I am saying is that words must be put together to indicate feeling which is more directly and powerfully expressed in action. We saw, when discussing the need for people to enact dramatically their roles, that words of love are no substitute for its demonstration by one person to another.

These ideas suggest that our bodies, and how we use them in our everyday relationships, have a communicative role which should not be seen as simply supporting language, because bodies have a different way of presenting or articulating things. The things which are presented in this way need not be abstract, artistic concepts; I am not suggesting that we are all artists in our everyday behaviour. And yet everything that Goffman has written about the need for people to convey an impression of poise, or good bearing or whatever style you will, depends upon precisely this ability to articulate an idea with our bodies. The widow who carries herself with dignity at her husband's funeral is credited by her fellow mourners for showing courage and control. This cannot be conveyed by her simply telling people that she must be brave, nor should she appear at the funeral smiling and confident. Instead, her portrayal of dignity depends upon the simultaneous expression of grief *and* its control; this is achieved through bodily conduct in a way irreducible to words alone. Words can evoke our experience of such things, but they cannot replace it. If we are to have explanations of how we communicate with our bodies, then we need a theory which embraces the special features of the problem that we seek to understand.

A reflection of society: an anthropologist's view of the body

In the previous section I introduced a view of bodily expression put forward by a philosopher. In the present one I want to take up some ideas about the body suggested by an anthropologist. What these writers have in common is a view of bodily expression which is broader than that upon which psychologists and communication theorists normally depend. In the case of Susanne Langer, this breadth of vision was achieved by looking at the body as a vehicle of aesthetic expression; in the case of Mary Douglas, her concern is with the body as reflecting something of the social order to which people belong.

Douglas (1971, 1973) noted that in different societies people have different degrees of control of their bodily expressions. In some societies this degree of control is relatively weak, so that (as with the pygmies) they might laugh by lying on the ground and kicking their legs in the air. In other societies, there is a greater control of bodily expression, so that laughing is an activity usually restricted to the face and vocal organs. The point she makes is that laughing (to take one example of non-verbal behaviour) cannot be understood by focusing upon the body alone, and certainly not by trying to isolate it upon one particular part of the body. Her argument is that societies (and groupings too, we must presume) set different thresholds for the body, so that in one culture the body is freely used, whereas in another it is more constrained. In the first case, people have more scope to move their bodies in the course of interaction, to gesticulate and to touch one another. This is true of people from the West Indies certainly as compared to people in Britain; for the latter a free and easy use of the body is seen as 'unrefined', and touching is relatively uncommon except between intimates (Jourard 1966). Douglas suggests that the difference between these two kinds of culture – one showing relatively weak, the other relatively strong control – reflects the fact that the physical body mediates the social structure to which it belongs. What she means by this is that the way in which people use their bodies reflects, or better still endorses, the norms of society.

Perhaps the above idea can be more readily illustrated by comparing the behaviour of people at funerals and at parties. Attending a funeral requires that the mourners conduct themselves with a quiet dignity, so that their physical bearing makes the occasion what it is. This means that gesticulating openly or talking enthusiastically is frowned upon; that is, the body is regarded as constrained in its use as a way of communicating. By comparison, at a party the people join in, not by making particular movements, but by being expansive and innovative in the use of the body. Of course, there are controls to party behaviour, but the endorsement of the atmosphere lies in the way that the guests 'join in the fun'. The difference between the two situations, as far as bodily conduct is concerned, lies not in what people do specifically, as in the scope which they have to communicate with their bodies.

It is on this basis that Douglas has criticized research which attempts to link social meanings to specific parts of the body (like hand movements) or to so-called channels of communication (like gaze). To study the body in this way, she argues, is to treat it like some sort of signal box, a static object which emits and receives strictly coded signals. In truth, however, this 'signal box' can 'fold down and straighten up, shake, dance or go into a frenzy' (1971). In effect, the specific movements which would retain their function if the body were static change their meaning according to the scope of its expressive use. To give an example, in church where the body may have little scope for expression, small movements of the face or hands made towards another person may carry a significance which would be entirely lost in the party setting. It is not the selection between a fixed set of gestures which provides variation in bodily communication, but the way in which the person acts in the context of the situation which his or her body helps to define. This is another way of recognizing Goffman's proposal that we check out what people say and do against the definition of self and situation which they put forward. The person who giggles in church and the person who greets a stranger with too warm a handshake are both contradicting the definition of the situation to which the remainder of their bodily conduct is evidence. This view of the body sees it as both complete (rather than a collection of separate channels), and as reflective of the social order which it helps to define.

7

THE SOCIAL BODY: INTIMACY
AND CONTROL

> Joe laid his hand upon my shoulder with the touch of a woman. I have
> often thought of him since, like the steam-hammer, that can crush a
> man or pat an eggshell, in his combination of strength with
> gentleness . . .
> O dear good Joe, whom I was so ready to leave and so unthankful to,
> I see you again, with your muscular blacksmith's arm before your eyes,
> and your broad chest heaving, and your voice dying away. O dear good
> faithful tender Joe, I feel the loving tremble of your hand upon my arm,
> as solemnly this day as if it had been the rustle of an angel's wing.

This quotation, taken from Dickens's *Great Expectations*, illustrates the
way in which feelings which we hold to be of the greatest significance are
communicated with the body. In the previous chapter it was argued that the
body articulates or sets out feelings in a way which is different from the
form given to them by words alone. Of course, the reader will immediately
want to point out that the above quotation, chosen for its evocative power,
is composed of words alone. What they point towards, however, is
knowledge that we have of the social world because we live through and
with our bodies. While there is the possibility of translation between the
realms of speech and action, the two are not reducible to each other; action
is not 'a language of movements' any more than speech is nothing more than
internalized gesture. Nevertheless speech and action are connected, both in
their genesis (how they evolved in the human species) and in the fact that we
speak and act together at one time (Vygotsky 1962).

In this chapter I want to discuss the way that the body is used to initiate,
maintain and change social relationships. This will involve an analysis of
how we use our bodies both to show intimacy and to control the form of the
interaction. These terms are chosen because they reflect two strands of

research into the way that non-verbal behaviour is employed by different groups of people (e.g. men and women). In addition, intimacy and control invite us to see two rather different functions of bodily communication, with implications for the book's argument that social life is, in an important way, ambiguous. In the previous chapter a distinction was made between research which took the system of non-verbal communication as its problem area and studies which have focused upon the function which non-verbal behaviour has within different kinds of social relationship. It is the latter line of enquiry which will form the focus of interest in this chapter.

The regulation of intimacy

One of the first studies to link intimacy and control in an experiment on non-verbal behaviour was carried out by the British social psychologists Argyle and Dean (1965). They selected eye contact for special attention, because the eye serves the function both of establishing an intimate exchange ('looking into each other's eyes') and of gathering information about the other person. The eye, therefore, both expresses and surveys, in the course of a single glance. Argyle and Dean proposed that establishing a proper and appropriate level of intimacy in a relationship involves not just the eye, but other channels of communication, such as facial expression and proximity to the other person. For example, when with their loved ones, people are literally close together and are used to looking at each other's faces in close proximity, perhaps while holding or touching one another. In more formal relationships, not only is physical communication likely to be very restricted (e.g. shaking hands) but the amount of eye contact is likely to be much reduced. Where one of these features is radically altered, we may see the others' being adjusted to compensate. For example, on the London underground trains, rush-hour passengers travel 'cheek-by-jowl' in a crush which places them in close bodily contact. In that situation, most travellers avert their eyes so as not to meet those of the people next to them, thus compensating for the enforced closeness of the journey. Argyle and Dean proposed a general form of this occurrence, stating that there is a tendency for intimacy to be maintained in a kind of equilibrium, so that disturbances to one non-verbal aspect will be compensated for by changes in another.

The experiment which they carried out involved subjects each having a discussion with a person whom they believed to be like them, but who was in fact a confederate of the experimenters. This person sat at varying distances from the subject, sometimes nearer (2 feet), sometimes further away (6 or 10 feet). The purpose of the study was to find out if the amount of eye contact established by the subjects would vary with the changing distance. One interesting extension to the study was the use of subjects and confederates of different sexes, allowing for an examination of the effect of gender/sexual attraction upon eye contact. The results of the study showed that, as expected, when subjects were made to sit closer to the confederate, their degree of eye contact diminished. It also showed that, across all distances, the greatest mutual eye contact was between two women, less between two men, and least between a man and a woman. These differences were most marked when the two people were placed closer together. In this last situation, all subjects tried to offset the effect of being in close proximity with a stranger; some leaned backwards in their chairs, others shaded their eyes with their hands or scratched their head, and all looked at the other person for only a small length of time.

Argyle and Dean concluded from these results that, while looking at the other person's face is important for seeking information (the other's response to what you are saying), it also plays an important part in the establishment of what they called an 'equilibrium position'. They saw this position as being appropriate and comfortable for the particular individuals having the conversation. It is established by means of a mutual but implicit exchange of non-verbal signals. Other experimenters have also observed this relationship between close proximity and the reduction of eye-contact, but whether this is an inevitable result is open to question (Kleinke 1986). The matter turns upon the way in which intimacy is defined and arranged for in the experiment.

In a later study (Breed 1972), different degrees of intimacy were expressed by the changing behaviour of the confederate, who in the high-intimacy condition leaned forward and gazed into the eyes of the subject. In the moderate condition, the confederate sat erect and made intermittent eye-contact, while in the low-intimacy condition s/he sat at an angle, leaned back and made eye-contact with the subject twice only. The effect of this was that subjects leaned forward and made more eye contact as intimacy increased. On the face of it, this appears to be a result contrary to that obtained by Argyle and Dean. However, the design of the two studies are at a tangent, so to speak. Where Argyle and Dean made large changes to the distance between confederate and subject, whose level of intimacy remained stable, Breed arranged that the confederates themselves would alter the level of intimacy expressed. This meant that Argyle and Dean's subjects found themselves placed nearer to another person whom they assumed to be a subject just like themselves. In contrast, those taking part in Breed's study were faced with someone (again, assumed to be just another subject) who 'made the running' in defining his or her approach to the relationship. While there might well be different equilibrium levels (of non-verbal behaviours) for relationships of differing intimacy, Breed's study showed that changes in the behaviour of one or both parties can alter the perceived intimacy of the relationship.

I shall, later on, discuss the way in which intimacy is signalled with the body, for this is one of the basic points which Argyle and Dean's study originally raised but never investigated. From what has just been pointed out about the research design, this issue could never be analysed in these terms because the authors appear to have worked without a definition of what intimacy involves. Breed's study reflected intimacy as something which is not simply a feature of one kind of relationship rather than another (e.g. husbands and wives are intimate: students and professors are not intimate). Instead, intimacy is held to be something that is expressed in people's changing behaviour and is open to interpretation by others. This is not to say that Argyle's and Dean's view of the function of non-verbal behaviour in this situation is incorrect; indeed, they are to be credited with making the point that eye contact serves both to intimate affection and to gather information. To forget this point is to lose one's bearings when surveying the many studies which have been carried out into non-verbal behaviour and the regulation of interaction.

These days there is a tendency to divide the field into behaviours which express intimacy and into those which regulate interaction. The former includes analyses of gazing by people who like each other to different degrees, while the latter includes things which are done as part of facilitating conversation. For example, it has been shown that people look away from the other person more when they are about to commence speaking, and towards the other person more when they are finishing what they have to say (Kendon 1967). Detailed analyses of conversations have shown a range of what have been called 'turn-yielding cues' which people use in the course of the give and take of everyday discussion. Perhaps because they are more readily observed, and because they are used by people without their knowledge, the place of such regulators in social interaction has taken up a disproportionate amount of research time. In spite of this, I shall not survey the many interesting findings concerning what people do or do not do as they speak, because they shed no light on the question of how the body expresses both intimacy and control at the same time. Indeed, if the regulators are considered by themselves, there is a lack of agreement about how they do function in social interaction (Beattie 1983). For example, gaze has been taken to be an indicator of expressed intimacy but it has also been shown to increase when people want to be persuasive or deceptive, as well as being seen as a demand for a response. Similarly, leaning forward whilst talking has been taken as an indicator of increased interest, but in some contexts it can appear as intrusive and rude. If you are preparing an essay in the library and find someone sitting closer while trying to look over your work, you might well stare at this intruder in order to ascertain just what is going on. Clearly there are differences in gaze which are only comprehensible with reference to the intentions of the participants and the context of the action.

The problem with attempts to define precisely how regulators should operate is that they are not context free or, to put it more simply, how the body is used and interpreted depends upon the situation. The reader who has read the previous pages will not be surprised by this proposal which appears as novel only if one limits oneself to a narrow range of examples of how people live their lives together (i.e. two-person conversations). If bodily communication depends upon context, then we should widen the range of examples that we take into consideration. In particular, we might consider situations in which intimacy and control are to be found together, for it is variation in the former which can so radically alter how the exchange between people is regulated. One interesting illustration may be taken from a study by Adam Kendon (1975) of a couple filmed kissing while sitting on a park bench. Kissing is, perhaps *par excellence*, an example of what can be termed intimate behaviour. I use the words 'what can be termed' because there is no behaviour that can be tagged with a label which defines it unambiguously. When discussing style in chapter 5, Goffman's example of different kinds of kissing (of marital affection, of friendly greeting) was introduced to make this point. In Kendon's study the act of kissing was studied from the structural perspective, so that the film of the couple's faces was analysed frame by frame, first to categorize and then to allocate each act to a patterned whole. What Kendon showed is that the sequence of kisses and embraces can be described in terms of the way that the couple offer, accept or refuse each other's facial displays. For example,

> Thus she turns to M [the man] with vigor and approaches him with 'fierce' faces. Yet, for but 9/24 of a second, just before their lips touch, F's [the woman's] face is posed for passionate, not for playful, kissing. Here, perhaps, she hints at passions someday (or sometime) to be aroused. Perhaps we see here an instance of what appears to be a common principle of courtship; the continued interest of the other partner is maintained, and even heightened by fleeting displays of behaviour that belong to later stages of the courtship program.

Notice that to distinguish between the different 'faces' which he observes, Kendon uses (I would say, must use) words like 'fierce', 'passionate' and 'playful' to give meaning to what would otherwise be facial movements lacking in social significance. His study shows that even intimate behaviour of this kind is subject to forms of regulations which the couple carry out together, without words but in a patterned way. What the analysis does not reveal, for it assumes it in its choice of subject, is what the couple express or say about their relationship in the course of their kissing. We understand the regulation of the interaction precisely because we know what kissing means, extending this knowledge to the couple involved. What Kendon's study shows is that intimate social behaviour is patterned and subject to control: what it does not address is how intimacy is established in the first place, so that the interaction has one form rather than another.

The point to be emphasized is that, in personal relationships, the body is a source of information about both the course of the exchange (who is to speak, when to break off) and about the level of intimacy which those involved assume towards one another. For example, a child tugging at its mother's sleeve is trying to alter her behaviour but does this within a relationship of dependent affection which the tug confirms, partly in its directness, partly in its smallness. By focusing upon the regulation of interaction (i.e. upon the control features) in studies which fix the level of intimacy for those taking part, one misses this question altogether. In effect, the problem becomes particularly interesting only when we begin to consider examples of social interaction where the level of intimacy cannot be easily assumed, where it is subject to fluctuation, or to irreversible change.

'Come closer': intimating personal relationships

From the discussion of Argyle and Dean's experiment, it seems that once a relationship is on a stable footing, a certain pattern of bodily behaviour is to be expected. The question remains, however, how do we establish or shift the basis of our relationships with particular individuals? The simple answer to this question is that often an invitation is offered which shows just what is intended (e.g. 'Would you like to go to the cinema this evening?' or 'How would you and Bob like to come round for dinner next Saturday?' or, more directly, 'Would you like to come up and see my etchings?'). The fact is that, even where explicit invitations are offered, they are often preceded by changes in the behaviour of one individual to the other. Sometimes these invitations come 'out of the blue' but more often than not they are justified by minor changes in the relationship which foreshadow them. These changes result in what we commonly call people's 'feeling more relaxed' with each other or 'getting on well' together. They are differences which involve people's actions, gestures and expressive behaviours. From studies of the way that people perceive changes in particular gestures or postures, there has built up a catalogue of the kind of specific actions deemed more likely to be seen by another person as 'signs of liking'. We have mentioned some already when considering gaze and posture. Another is touch, as was shown in a study where some subjects were touched lightly on the hand by a library assistant as they returned their identification card (Fisher, Rytting and Heslin 1976). It was found afterwards that those individuals who were touched liked the assistant more than those who were not touched, and that this made them feel better into the bargain. What is notable about this finding is that the subjects did not have to realize that they had been touched for this effect to work.

This experiment is an example of the way that people intimate closeness in their everyday relationships. I use the verb 'intimate' to show that it is something done implicitly, without being spoken out loud. We make changes *to* the way in which our bodily communications will be interpreted *by means of* bodily action. This is not so very different from what was discussed in chapter 5 as the way that the body is used to frame relationships. There we examined the way in which a playful episode might be invoked by a particular (e.g. 'silly') posture or facial expression. Here I am drawing attention to the way that we invite a change in the basis of the relationship by offering, as it were, examples from what we and the other might share (Scheflen 1965). This might include such things as standing closer to the person, putting a hand on their arm and almost certainly smiling or using our faces to 'show our feelings'. These particulars are meant to be illustrative of what is, in fact, a disposition of the body as a whole, for the use of one behaviour in the absence of the others may be taken as a sign of insincerity or of other motives (e.g. touching, especially of women by men). There is, therefore, an inevitable uncertainty about these exchanges; they are, as many people have found to their cost, somewhat risky. The risk may be small, meaning that the smile is not returned, the arm is withdrawn or the other person fails to respond to the overture being made. Because such bodily changes are made more or less spontaneously, and because they are open to interpretation by the other person, their meaning is there to be determined by the other's response or lack of it. The point is that, while we might study the signals which are normally seen as being overtures of friendship or love, we cannot say with any certainty that they always elicit the response for which they were made. The meaning of a gesture or facial expression is not wrapped up within it.

This view of bodily communication shows that, while we may enjoy relationships with established levels of formality, there is a precariousness about social life into which we can be steered by such things as a meeting of eyes, leading, say, to a sexual liaison. The rules which operate to channel and to limit bodily conduct in social situations are not inviolable, and even the presentation of self is not wholly secure, in that we give off information to be read by others. This does not mean that we are prey to our bodily expressions; we are still aware, through moral codes, of how we are expected to behave. When someone makes what is seen as an invitation to intimacy which is inappropriate, the person to whom this is directed can make clear signs of withdrawal, perhaps indicating refusal *and* flattery at the proposal, and not an explicit word said on the matter. In fact, flirting between people who are attached to other partners can be enjoyable, not only for the pleasures of mutual attraction, but also because it can be done well. By this I mean that the allusions which are made using expression and gesture, by both parties, steer a fine course between passion and restraint, impropriety and acceptability, vulgarity and good taste.

The above example is also an illustration of the fact that communications of intimacy do not take place between individuals who are isolated, but between people who are in otherwise public situations, where the scope for bodily expression may be limited by the norms of the group. Between people who are already close (say, husband and wife), expressions of intimacy are expected, though to be tempered by a concern for others present. Between people who are trying to get to know one another better, the situation is different in that their gestures may need to be made so that they are not visible to the others present. In chapter 2 the question of visibility was raised in relation to the formation of appearances, so that a wink or a frown made to one person only might carry a meaning which it would not convey were the same gesture to be made in the sight of all present. This shade of secrecy attaching to the communication gives it its meaning, accentuated when carried out in circumstances where it might be inappropriate. For example, the man who winks at a woman at a dinner party, while the host is telling a story, simultaneously risks appearing rude to the company and chancing an extension of his relationship with her through this 'secret sign'. The point is that we cannot hope to understand what is going on in such exchanges without broadening our view from a study of gesture alone to action in the group context.

Bodily communication, status and gender differences

We have seen that some of the earliest studies of bodily expressions were carried out as comparisons between people of different cultures. As the investigation of non-verbal communication became more detailed, so these details became, in their turn, the basis of further group comparisons. Among these, the paralinguistic behaviours of whites and blacks were compared, showing that they have different patterns of looking while talking and listening (LaFrance and Mayo 1976). The interaction distance chosen by men of different rank has been investigated, showing that, when addressing a superior, the distance is greater the more the discrepancy in rank (i.e. a lieutenant will stand further away from a general than from a captain (Dean, Willis and Hewitt 1975). These comparisons lend significance to the gestures studied because, it is argued, they reflect something about the status differences of the people concerned. So, in the studies mentioned above, the different gaze pattern of blacks is cited as a possible cue open to misinterpretation by whites during conversation, it being assumed that, in most interactions of this kind, black people will be dependent upon the goodwill of whites.

There has been no greater interest in bodily conduct differences than those between men and women. This is not only because of an abiding concern with matters sexual (see some of the popular books on body language), but also because of the questions raised by writers concerned with feminism and gender. Before considering this topic in more detail, we should note that the studies which are included in it are thought of as having more to do with control than with intimacy. At the beginning of this chapter I pointed out that control and intimacy are the two strands of work upon which it would focus. It was suggested that the two functions are often coexistent in what people do; we cannot always point separately to gestures done to control and to those done to show affection. In fact, the difference between these two features of bodily conduct is made wider by the approaches of the researchers involved. In one review social control and intimacy were contrasted in terms of people's motivations (Edinger and Patterson 1983). The authors argued that social control (through non-verbal behaviour) is defined as 'attempting to influence or change the behaviour of another person', while intimacy (expressed non-verbally) is a 'spontaneous manifestation of an affective reaction towards the other person'. What this suggests is that our bodies provide two clearly different things. On the one hand our expressions are eruptions of raw feeling, while on the other our gestures are contrivances to make other people do things that they would not do of their own accord.

From what has been said already in this book, this position is one which falls painfully short of providing the student with a realistic view of social life. As Langer (1957) has said, people may be influenced through feelings executed with grace, tenderness or devotion (see again the quotation which heads this chapter).

One major, and commonly referred to, difference in the way that men and women use their bodies is walking. In an early paper the French sociologist Marcel Mauss (1972) observed that cinema usherettes in Paris adopted the walk of American actresses whom they had watched on the screen. His point was that walking is not a biological activity, something controlled from within our physiology, but is a learned technique adopted by different groups in distinct ways. Men can, and some do, walk in a way that is the cultural norm for women. Similarly, some women walk in a way that is more typical of men in Western society. The study of gender differences in bodily behaviour is not, therefore, a study in 'sex differences', but rather one of how members of different social groups have adopted, and maintained, different ways of conducting themselves when in each other's presence, and with individuals of their own gender. As with the discussion in chapter 6 regarding informative and communicative behaviour, we ought to avoid thinking of all behaviours which are typical of a group as communications which individual members intend. Indeed, the arguments which arise in everyday life as to whether women 'ask for' the unwanted sexual attentions of men turn upon confusions about the status of gestures and postures.

Nancy Henley (1977) summarized research on gender differences in a book titled *Body Politics: Power, Sex and Nonverbal Communication*. The book's title reflects her thesis that women use styles of bodily behaviour which are coded in our society as indicating a status subordinate to that held by men. She argues, for example, that in the use of space, men expand into it while women are more restrained and restricted. Men sit on a park bench and spread out, put their arms along the seat back and stretch their legs; women sit on the bench with knees together and arms tucked into their body. This is an observation only, but supported by studies showing that American women carry their bodies and limbs together, 'as a whole', while American men use their arms in a way where they are held out from the body. Perhaps this explains the finding of one study of American college students which showed that, while walking across campus, the women held their books to the front of their bodies (across the chest), while the men held them in their hands, swinging by their side (Jenni and Jenni 1976). However, whether all differences between men and women in their use of space can be regarded as a control function, in the sense of being intended by one group to curtail the actions of the other, is debatable. That there are such differences, and that they are knowingly used by some men to dominate women in certain situations, is undoubtedly true.

The effect of touch on people's perceptions of each other has already been mentioned. In the study of what happened when library assistants touched users, one ambivalent finding was that touched females also saw the library itself more positively, but the opposite was the case for males (Fisher *et al.* 1976). Indeed, the study of touch suggests that to understand what is happening we need to distinguish between different kinds of touch, different intentions which in-form the way that the body is used. In her review of touching between people in public situations, Henley concludes that touching is something done more by superiors than by subordinates and reviews evidence to show that men touch women more than women touch men. However, within the sexes there is a different distinction, in that it is socially acceptable for women to touch each other (e.g. to walk arm in arm), but not so for men. In the case of men, touch is ritualized in the handshake and in stylized contact such as grasps of the shoulder.

It would seem, therefore, that touch, like posture and proximity, is indicative of differences in the access which individuals of different status have to one another. Henley's argument is that this status difference applies to men and women, and that the broad sweep of non-verbal communication that we see (and execute) in public is testimony to this fact. She adds to this the difference in the way that men and women make eye contact in public places. There is a tendency for the man to look at the woman, and for the latter to avert her gaze. This, Henley argues, is indicative of the status which society accords to men as the active partner in the gender relationship, and to women as the passive partner. Women, on the whole, feel observed more than men do and have been found (in an experimental situation) to rate men whom they think have stared at them as less attractive (Kleinke, Bustos, Meeker and Staneski 1973). A somewhat different pattern of behaviour has been found when examining the conversations of men and women together. In several studies it has been shown that women look at the other person (whether man or woman) more than men do, both while talking and listening. If the normal visual feedback is artificially interrupted (say by using a screen), then women show greater signs of discomfort than men. When this happens in mixed-sex conversations, it is the man who tends to dominate while the woman takes up a passive role, of the person who is observed (Argyle, Lalljee and Cook 1968).

Before turning to a possible explanation of this difference, we should note that there is strong evidence that women are better than men at making the correct interpretation of other people's non-verbal communications (Hall 1978). This evidence comes mainly from experimental studies asking subjects to make judgements about filmed or recorded performances of chosen emotions; they are therefore not of women and men who are actually involved in a real-life relationship. An exception to this form of design was one study in which members of married couples were asked to send ambiguous messages to each other, and for each to guess what the other had communicated non-verbally (Noller 1980). It was confirmed that wives were more able to 'decode' accurately the messages sent by their spouses than husbands were able to do. There was a difference, however, between positive and negative communications, particularly when sent by husbands to wives. Husbands had trouble sending positive messages, which their wives were much better at communicating. This was somewhat confounded by the fact that wives tended to overestimate the amount of positive feeling that their husbands sent. One possible explanation is that men are perhaps less expressive, so that where husbands sent even a little positive feeling, this was used by the wife as evidence of an overall positive message.

How do we account for these findings? One explanation which has been put forward proposes that women's role in society has been to facilitate the life of their menfolk. This has required women to be more attentive to the moods and needs of the men in their families. They have, therefore, been socialized to be more accommodating to men. In the course of conversation this means being attentive to the expressions and the dispositions of their partners. This openness to cues might be facilitated by the fact that women smile more than men do; as a result, women might express a readiness to accept the opinions of men, or at least be sensitive to their moods and attitudes. However, the authors of what has been called the accommodation hypothesis (Rosenthal and DePaulo 1979) have placed a caveat on the superiority of women as interpreters of bodily cues. They point out that, while a sensitivity to the main cues (e.g. facial expression) will be advantageous, should women focus upon fleeting or minor cues, they risk the chance of misinterpreting what has been said.

We might sum up this inequality by saying that in their bodily conduct men reassert their power to initiate changes in the relationship, and women reassert their determination to prevent or to allow this to happen. Consistent with the point made in the previous chapter, I am not arguing that either individual men or women intend, in every case, to communicate this state of affairs. In their different bodily styles, men and women are like two different sub-cultures. Using the ideas of Langer and Douglas, we can say that the bodies of men and women articulate (or make manifest) differences in the controls which are embodied in social norms. The bodily communications of the sexes can be viewed as the display, in dramatic form, of rules which are otherwise difficult to envisage. However, as with all rules, these are best shown when they are not followed strictly but are bent a little, and occasionally broken. Society works through us, if you like, and we lend ourselves to or resist its direction where we are aware of this, as we are able, and as we wish.

With the above points in mind, the student should beware of seeing this comparison of men and women as one of 'non-verbal behaviours' which are used solely for the two groups' mutual control. These different ways of using the body also form the repertoire upon which men and women must draw when showing affection for one another. (This demonstration of affection is not limited to sexual relationships; see the quotation at the head of the chapter.) There is a danger in interpreting all bodily conduct as being just social control, based upon generalizations from the study of strangers meeting under the scrutiny of social scientists. What particular gestures, done by particular people, in particular contexts mean, cannot be settled by fiat. We have seen that these things are open to debate, to reinterpretation, to error and to deception. Questions of intimacy and control, particularly in sexual relationships, are inseparable. Getting to know a person of the opposite sex whom one is attracted to demands the use of control, in the form of charm or flattery or gentle persuasion. The direct and unrestrained expression of attraction (seen as love or lust) is unlikely to meet with success. Similarly, seducing a member of the opposite sex will usually require some intimation of affection, though this is not put forward as a general rule. The reader should note that these remarks are not intended to water down the points made about gender, bodily signals and power. I have stressed that these are socially structured ways of using the body and do not vanish every time members of the opposite sex declare a personal relationship. (Kendon's (1975) study of kissing shows this to be true.) But we can know only how they are being employed, where they are being altered and when they are being resisted by making descriptions of particular contexts. Men and women are members of other groups too, of social classes, of professions and of neighbourhoods. We saw in chapter 4 how multiple group membership matters in the formation of a person's social identity, and therefore in the way in which that will be expressed in bodily conduct. In the next section we shall examine bodily expression as an aspect of style, something characteristic of identity arising from the role of groups in society.

Bodily communication and group identity: the use of style

In the earlier chapters of this book there have been references to group structure, to group identity and to group ethos. By the last term I mean something along the lines of the culture of the group which the outsider discerns through the pattern of life which the group members share, something giving expressive form to their social and material life experience. I have in mind here the youth sub-cultures which have emerged in Britain over the last thirty years or so, the Teddy Boys of the 1950s, the Mods and Rockers of the 1960s and the emergence of Punk in the 1970s. One of the reasons for choosing these groups is that they were each distinguishable by appearance and by style of behaviour. The other reason is that they can all be seen as relatively subordinate groups whose members were often drawn from the working class and whose behaviour came to be seen as opposing the traditional values of the older-adult majority. In this section I want to use these examples to show how bodily communication can be considered as something much wider than the control of conversation. Viewed as style, it is something that we can understand as deriving from groupings in society, and as something which maintains distinctions between people through the making of appearances (Hebdige 1979).

One example of such a group was studied by Willis (1975), who described a group of 'motor-bike boys' who lived in Birmingham. Their bikes were at the centre of their activities. What is interesting about this is the differences between these boys' use of the bike from that of the usual motorcyclist:

> To start with, helmets and goggles were never worn . . . [they] . . . destroy the excitement of the wind rushing into the face, and of the loud exhaust-beat thumping the ears. The point of fast driving was the experience, not the fact, of speed . . . (p. 235)

> The motor-bike boy is in the 'world out there' and copes with handling his motor-bike at the same time as feeling the full brunt of its movement in the natural physical world. . . . Jackets are partly open and are not buttoned down around the throat, belts are not worn, there's nothing to keep the jacket close to the skin, trousers are not tucked away in boots and socks, there is nothing to prevent wind tunneling up the sleeves. Adornments of the jacket and free-flowing neckties add, although fractionally, to the total drag, an unnecessary drag that would be avoided by conventional motor-cyclists . . . . (pp. 236–7)

Willis describes the group's members as adopting a style of moving confidently in a very physical and a very masculine world. Based upon the use of the motor-bike, the excitement and the associated physical perils, this style extended into their other leisure activities, including their love of raucous music. The quotation given above shows that one important aspect of their style was the deliberate avoidance or undoing of clothing associated with conventional (safer) motor-cyling. This simultaneously allowed them to experience the ride with their bodies in a way denied to the conventional rider, and to make a symbolic display of this to onlookers. These are two important points, one relating more to the internal dynamics of the group and one more to the relationship of the group to the majority culture. The experience of the ride was something which they shared together and which was a focus of the group's activity; the display of their riding on the public highway or their meetings at roadside cafés proclaimed the values of the group, which contrasted with those of the people who surrounded them. This bodily style was evoked through riding the bikes in a way which deliberately broke the conventional rules, and through conducting themselves in an exaggerated masculine way which threatened always to breach the rules of 'polite society'. Willis is at pains in his discussion, however, to point out that this style was more than mere violence: it permeated all the things which group members did in public, being a 'confidence in movement' which coloured action, expanding it into a rough kind of bonhomie.

There are three points which we can draw from this illustration to show how a discussion of the body is tied up with earlier concerns about appearances and social groups. First, a direct comparison can be drawn between these riders and the ones who were referred to in chapter 5 when discussing style (Goffman 1961). Those riders, the children and youths on wooden fairground horses, were also described as being involved in the evocation of style, though for themselves rather than in a group. In either case, the body is deployed around the horse or upon the bike in such a way as to show that the person is more than a rider in the conventional sense. This is not done by means of special gestures which, in themselves, mean protest or the willingness to take risks. One cannot discern, upon the body itself (i.e in the person's 'non-verbal behaviour'), the meaning which the style denotes. Instead, one has to understand the rider in the context of the conventional way of riding, and to do this requires some knowledge of the physical situation in which the person's body is deployed.

This brings us on to the second point, that bodily style is not something achieved in abstraction from the material world. The kind of youth groups which were mentioned at the beginning of this section are most easily identifiable to the majority of people by their clothes; for example, the Teddy boys by the long jackets with suede collars and suede shoes, the punks by the torn clothing and the hairpin stuck in the earlobe or through the nostril. Willis too, noted that when the motor-bike boys played football they avoided doing this in appropriate clothing. How one moves, how the body is either more constrained or loosened in its ability to make gestures, is channelled by the clothes which are worn and the environment in which the group chooses to meet. In chapter 3 we saw that the environment made demands upon groups which, as they meet them, established what Homans (1951) called 'external systems of relationships'. There it was noted that not only do groups respond to their environment, but they also fashion it, so that their pattern of friendships ('internal system') can direct the kind of places in which they want to meet, the kind of technical artefacts they wish to exploit (e.g. bikes, 'ghetto-blaster' radios) and the organization of property ownership and sharing. The summary point is that bodily communication, considered as style, cannot be understood by looking at movement in an abstract world, as if communication was by hands and faces moving, as was said before, in some psychological ether.

The third point to be drawn from this illustration is that the motor-bike boys formed a group which distinguished itself from other groups. Indeed, one of the marks of all the youth cultures mentioned above is that they express, in different ways, some kind of revolt against the majority. This does not mean that they existed apart from the dominant culture, for they shared in this to the extent that they were the sons, daughters, sisters and brothers of people who, in turn, did not share their special interests (Clarke,

Hall, Jefferson and Roberts 1976). That is to say, they were members of multiple groups, located at the intersect of class, family and neighbourhood. We have seen that social identity is established in the matrix of group relationships where individuals stand, as it were, at the crossing of the groups to which they simultaneously belong. As part of this intersection, there will be groups which are dominant and those which are subordinate. When discussing these matters earlier on, I said that one of the ways that subordinate groups express themselves (in the sense of expressing a group identity) is to revolt against the standards set by the majority. For youth groups such as Skinheads or Punks, their social identity was achieved through an expressive style based upon an inversion of the values of the majority culture. Again, this was not an abstract process but was achieved through transformations in dress and adornment (the boots of the Skinheads, the hairstyles of the Punks). This is as if to say, 'What the majority do, we do the opposite,' or 'Where the majority find meaning, we make nonsense.'

The key to understanding these body styles lies in seeing that they are responses *within* a culture *to* that culture. We saw in chapter 4 that the subordinate group is often condemned to make its gestures in the terms dictated by the majority group, and they often appear as 'mere gestures' for that reason. Yet, to reaffirm a point already made, the body can be a powerful medium for communicating relationship. The child who belches at the table, the schoolchildren who fart in class or the student who affects boredom are all exploiting the fact that such small breaches of bodily conduct comment upon the situation, without easily being made the subject of discussion by those in authority. This does not mean that this is all that dissenting bodily styles do; they also serve to provide a focus for the affirmation of a common identity by the group members.

Not surprisingly, these deliberate displays of opposing bodily styles are met with condemnation by the dominant culture, for whom they appear as not merely different but as threatening the 'ordinariness', the 'taken for grantedness', the 'naturalness' of life which makes it seem worthwhile. We are back, here, to questions which we addressed briefly in chapter 2 concerning appearances in social life. The establishment of distinct bodily styles by youth groups is, in part, aided by the labels which they are accorded by the majority who observe them. These labels might not be very complimentary; they might not accord with the group members' own reasons for why they act as they do, but they contribute to the group's being given its own identity and to certain aspects of its dress and behaviour as being singled out as typical of its style. Where these aspects of behaviour are in direct opposition to the majority's values (such as with 'football-fan violence'), then there will be action to curtail the group (Marsh *et al* 1978). Where, on the other hand, people in general do not see or care about a group's style of conduct (as was the case with the motor-bike culture), then these behaviours are less open to manipulation by the dominant culture (Wilson 1978).

In summary, the expressive styles which sub-groups adopt are formed in the intersections of the different groups to which people belong. The form of these bodily styles needs to be understood as expressive of the relationships between groupings which are often of unequal status and power. The body, thought of as a medium for articulating a way of life, needs to be understood in terms such as these; it cannot be treated as an isolated signal-box (or even two such boxes coupled together) which it has often been in research to date.

8

IDEAS IN PRACTICE:
THE DENIAL OF AMBIGUITY

The idea that ambiguity is basic to social relations has been a thread running through our discussion of groups and of social interaction. In this final chapter I want to show what happens to our understanding of social life when psychologists either fail to see or try to avoid the ambiguities which we have noted. Having done this, we will be able to go back to some of the main ideas presented in the book to show what kind of intellectual approach they signify. After all, I did say at the outset that this book is not a neutral survey of the field. In truth, no such survey exists, for all reviews assume some basic approach to the subject matter. In this book the broad approach has been to tip the balance towards the phenomenon to be explained. This has been done through the use of examples wherever possible, setting these alongside the findings of experiment and formal inquiry. Added to this, I have selected, for discussion, authors whose work is sympathetic to this approach, and who have preserved the uncertainties of social life in their accounts and in their theories. If one was to summarize the argument very briefly, it could be said that the book has put a question mark against the assumption that 'selves', 'group' and 'gestures' are the ready-made building blocks for constructing explanations of social life. From even the brief survey possible in the foregoing chapters, it should be clear that psychologists (and others) have often begun with just this assumption. Staying with this line of thinking means that one continues to study these things as if they had, indeed, a separate existence in the real world of people's lives. I hope that the examples which we have considered so far, and those thought of by the reader along the way, have shown that this is more of an expedient for academics than it is a reflection of everyday life.

The book has put forward the following arguments. The identities which individuals claim for themselves are not inner personalities, but matters of appearance; the groups to which people belong are not circumscribed containers, but merging and emerging standpoints for action; the gestures which we make do not each carry fixed, separate meanings but are fashioned in the course of acting with style. Before reviewing the approach which the book has been assembling, let us look at one consequence of treating social interaction as if it were made up of relatively fixed elements which are supposedly put together in an unambiguous fashion.

Meeting an immense human need? Training people in social skills

I have taken the words for this section's heading from a paper by Michael Argyle (1984), in which he reviews the enormous growth in the application of what has come to be called 'social-skills training'. The concept of social skill came from a comparison of non-verbal behaviour with the actions of people doing things such as typing or riding a bicycle. In the 1950s psychologists had adopted the ideas of feedback and control (the principle of the 'feedback loop') to analyse adaptive and habituated behaviour as 'skill'. Skill involves the performer in seeking certain goals, making adaptive moves, observing what effect one is having, and taking corrective action as necessary in the light of the 'feedback' available. Argyle (1973) argued that this idea of practical skill is analogous to the skills of individuals when engaged in conversation or other forms of interaction. In this way, the meshing of head nods and eye contact which regulate the course of a conversation show skill; helping the other person out of a potentially embarrassing situation shows skill; putting other people at their ease shows skill; striking up a conversation with someone whom you find attractive shows skill; chairing a committee meeting needs skill; selling goods or products or the company's good name demands skill, and so on. I have deliberately listed this variety of activities to show the range of things which could come under this general term.

The use of the skills terminology has, as one of its effects, the rendering of all the various facets of social life into a single form, a single kind of 'stuff' that they are composed of. Once everything that people do can be understood in this way, it is possible to approach every situation, every person and every activity as if it were a composite of such skills. By analysing these aspects of social life into their relative 'skill components' it becomes possible to see how people might be helped to improve their behaviour to become more skilled. Should they be shy, or unable to make friends, or ineffective at work – in effect, inadequate – then they might be helped to alter their behaviour in order to be seen by others to be more effective people. Indeed, social-skills training has been applied by psychologists in many of life's arenas; in the clinic to those called neurotic, in training those whose work requires that they be 'skilled' in dealing with people, and to members of the general public who want to be either more assertive or successful with the opposite sex (Trower, Bryant and Argyle 1978). I am not going to draw the reader into a debate about how well these training methods work, because that matter is secondary to the issue of how interaction comes to be seen in this way, and what effect it can have upon our thinking about social life (Ellis and Whittington 1981; Wilkinson and Canter 1982). In particular, I want to argue that treating conduct as a skill depends upon a denial of the ambiguity that is central to social life. While this might not matter to individuals who benefit from the training (committees get chaired more effectively, girls/boys are dated more easily), it should matter to students of social interaction. For they might, if they are not vigilant, take the metaphor of skill (as currently employed) to be the reality of human behaviour.

What does social-skills training involve? There are many variants of the basic theme, but all depend upon the analysis of the 'skill' to be changed and upon the designation of the goal of training. For example, helping someone who finds it difficult to cope with social situations might involve an analysis of the degree of difficulty he or she finds when going to parties, being with a group of the opposite sex or looking someone directly in the eyes (Trower *et al* 1978). Notice that people's responses in these situations and what they are aiming to achieve depend upon their notions of what is expected and how they think they appear to others. The situations are subject to norms and to conventions, and the individual's behaviour (both before and after training) to their intentions. These are not ignored by trainers but are taken into account; they must be, because the criteria for a 'skilled performance' depend precisely upon these social evaluations. This should cause us no surprise, for we have seen that social interaction involves people in claims born of group membership. For that reason, we understand, in common-sense terms, why a person from an underprivileged background will see his or her opportunities (to speak in a certain way, to adopt a style of behaviour) relative to those of the rich and the successful. Whatever social skills may be, they rest upon a whole system of value judgements which have their origin in society and are reflected in our individual behaviours. Social skills cannot be value free; they are only meaningful in terms of social norms and the intentions of the individuals concerned. Oddly enough, it is these two aspects of non-verbal behaviour which, as we have seen, are often missing from the experimental study of non-verbal behaviours.

To cast social interaction as a set of social skills and to train people in its more effective use are part and parcel of being a professional psychologist. I do not mean that all psychologists are trainers, but that we cannot understand social skills without realizing that it involves the application of knowledge by experts (Radley 1985). Is this a new occurrence? In one sense it is not, given that, for a long time, there have been experts who advised others on the correct or acceptable forms of behaviour in company. A review of advice to gentlefolk from medieval times onwards shows that the niceties of deportment were taken very seriously (Wildeblood 1973). It also shows that the way in which people behave together is tied up with the changing patterns of social structure. What would be regarded as proper, or polite, or rude takes its meaning from the groups to which people belong and to the norms of behaviour which are attached in each case. There is, in addition, a point which we need to grasp here about the relationship of the behaviour to the individuals in question. Where in courtly society, and in its echoes in the centuries which followed, polite conduct was seen as part of a person's social-group membership, in modern times 'stylish' or 'smooth' behaviour is taken as a mark of the individual's own personality (Berger, Berger and Kellner 1974). The course of social change is marked by a trend towards individualism, in which each of us is made relatively free of the social groups to which we belong in order to establish our individuality (our personality, our dignity) in the market-place of interpersonal dealings. This was not the case in past times, where one's social group membership included one's ways of behaving and limited the scope for change. Today there is a popular belief that people can aspire to be almost anything in society and, by working on themselves as well as at their job, can be almost any kind of personality. By attention to one's clothes, manner, tastes and friends it is possible to fashion a lifestyle which will add up to a richer, fuller social life. One's social manner is part of this, something upon which it is possible to work and to make more fitting or effective. What began as a potential for change has now become something which we should all desire. We are told that 'we pick up bad habits of perception and interpretation . . . [with] . . serious gaps in our repertoires of skills. . . We simply stop trying to improve ourselves' (Soucie 1979: 213). The possibilities for self-presentation which emerged from changes in social structure have become today the moral requirements for everyone who wants to be regarded as a responsible citizen.

This is the background against which we need to see social-skills training and, indeed, the popular interest in social interaction and in 'body codes'. Human relationships are not, essentially, social skills. They are seen as such only in the context of the need for individuals to establish their desired identities in the eyes of other people. One 'needs' social skills to 'present oneself more effectively', to be 'liked more readily', to 'hold the interest of others'; skills bridge the gap between what one is and what one wants to be for others. The role of psychologists who act as trainers is to facilitate this way of thinking and to bring about change in the desired direction. Perhaps that is why the people who are often seen as most suitable for social-skills training are the mentally ill, the sexually rejected and the gauche. The idea of the person (the generalized individual) as someone who has or lacks social skills is therefore a relatively modern invention. Underlying this idea is the emergence of psychology as a practical discipline, helping individuals in our society to be content and efficient (Rose 1989). In saying this we have at last come full circle in our argument – the society which people make through their interactions itself makes the images of personality which individuals use to fashion their appearances.

Findings by permission

The preceding chapters have depended upon argument and description as well as upon the authority of experimental findings. To readers familiar with psychology texts which rest upon the results of experiments alone, this might have seemed at times a dangerously subjective (if not arbitrary) way to go about things. I hope that by this stage of the book the choice of approach will have been justified; we have been able to entertain a variety of issues and a range of problems which are rarely discussed together. There is another reason for not wanting to introduce the subject of social interaction via the fruits of experiment exclusively. Experimenters usually assume that what they are studying is real; by this I mean that they treat the behaviours or perceptions of the subjects as the 'things' which either have to be explained, or which alter in ways which predict what will happen as a consequence. The approach taken in this book has been quite different to this, in that we have taken behaviour to be of a ceremonial kind, to borrow Goffman's term once again. This means that what people do in the course of their relationships cannot be understood in terms of 'cause and effect' psychology. Individuals act for reasons which they have and, sometimes even, they act to find a reason for what they do (Smail 1984). These reasons are part and parcel of what are generally regarded as motives, to be sure, but we have seen that motives spring from attributions and appearances which have their origin in society. The ring slipped on to the third finger of the left hand does not 'cause' the man to be faithful to his wife or vice versa. We have seen that the meaning of such actions lies in ritual which has symbolic form. As a further step, it has been argued that individual action, though socially patterned, is open-ended. The meaning of an action is not, as pointed out, wrapped up within it, because that meaning will emerge partly in terms of an indeterminate reply. When studying social relationships we are not confronted with facts, if we mean by this the predictable relationships of 'selves' and 'groups' and 'behaviours'. This does not mean that psychologists have not tried to treat social life in this way, devising experiments which try to show which 'factors' contribute to people doing or feeling particular things.

There are, however, important differences between the facts that experiments can relate and the nature of social life. One way to think of this is to remind ourselves of the tripartite classification introduced in chapter 5. There it was proposed that social behaviour can be thought of as being either drama, ritual or routine. These terms were defined in terms of the experience of the actor but broadly speaking came down to whether the action was novel (and therefore uncertain), regulated by convention or carried out habitually. A similar distinction has been drawn between different approaches in social science which see behaviour as either politics, ritual or fact (Robinson 1984). Politics is expressed through dialogue and can be seen wherever people argue and struggle to exert their will over others. It leads to outcomes which can be anticipated but not predicted with certainty. For example, an argument breaks out in a group about which method its members should use for electing a leader. One view will prevail and another will be eliminated. Nobody can know which method will be adopted, although it will set the structure of the group in the future. This structure is something which can be viewed more readily, since it involves the group members in adopting certain roles and behaviours in their dealings with one another. The patterning of these behaviours can be called ritualistic, meaning that the meaning of what the group members do is to be understood in terms of the group norms. Note that no study of the group norms alone will tell us about how they were established. Should we wish to know this, then we need to obtain some record of the dialogue which brought them about. Moreover, within the group's way of dealing with its work, certain events or aspects of people's behaviour appear so stable as to be called facts. And yet, from even an introduction to social science, we know that we must be cautious when using this word. 'Facts' are what people agree to call things. Within the norms of the group it may be a fact that Peter always copies Paul, but we would be wary of saying that Paul 'causes' Peter to do these things, meaning that this is an immutable fact. Instead, we would want to say that within the framework of the group Peter and Paul have a relationship in which their behaviours are interrelated, in a ritual fashion. This is the form of argument which we used in previous chapters when discussing the patterning of behaviour. Situations and events that social scientists study are not out there as 'matters of fact' but 'by permission', as a result of tacit agreement or overt choice.

What does this phrase, 'by permission', mean? Robinson (1984), who used these words, illustrated them by reference to the work of Bales, amongst others. He pointed out that Bales carried out his studies of decision-making in groups using the model of natural science; i.e. he collected data as if he was studying facts. As a consequence, his findings suggest that it is simply true (a fact) that if groups of people meet they will talk in such a way that certain outcomes follow. (To be fair, Bales also discussed the groups in which his predictions were not supported, but he could not adequately account for them within his theory.) Robinson suggests that the finding of the dual-status order is the chosen index (treated as a fact) of the ritual of decision-making which some (but not all) of these groups adopted. In chapter 3 we reinterpreted Bales's findings along such lines, talking of claims made by individuals rather than of leaders. If the form of the group discussion is the disguised ritual in Bales's work, where is the politics? Robinson says that the political aspect lies, as it always must do in such research, outside the boundaries of the experiment. He suggests that the use of all-male groups will have meant that the meetings ran on the basis of an ideology which accepted a hierarchy of participation, i.e. that there will be leaders and led. This is a political decision, in the terms used here, and to the extent that it seemed the proper way to go about things, a shared and a tacit one. Robinson compares this ideology with the experience of some all-women groups who have rejected the inequality of participation in favour of the group encouraging its less articulate members (for a review of this topic, see Bartol and Martin 1986). That is to say, the whole basis of what the group is trying to achieve can be questioned, and in so doing the rituals which flowed from its original form will be altered. Similarly, we saw in the attempt to apply Bales's work in contexts outside the laboratory (the committee, the family) that matters which appeared to be taken for granted by Bales simply cannot be so.

The conclusion to be drawn from this is that the study of social interaction is always the study of ritual and rests upon political or ideological considerations which single studies cannot easily comment upon. The use of experiments, particularly those carried out in the laboratory, excludes these matters. As a consequence, the relationship of the measures taken are given a stability which works for the experimental situation but not necessarily for situations in the outside world. This does not mean that experiments cannot tell us anything important. What it does mean, for the student of social relationships, is that there is the danger of seeing these results as being 'really factual' because the ritualistic context is hidden by the way that the study is reported. This is the reason why we have not approached this introduction through such reports; in the end, matters of appearance (and of politics) defy such studies and cannot be addressed through them. Appearances and rituals are matters of claim and counter-claim, of agreement and of dispute. It is in these areas of everyday life that ambiguity is part and parcel of our dealings with each other; to exclude, deny or push them to one side is to make one's study of people something which, in truth, it is not.

In everyday life, facts, rituals and politics are interwoven. People have arguments about what they should do within the pattern of their relationships, calling attention to matters which they might agree upon as facts. Let us make use once more of the example which introduced the book. The scenario was of a woman, Mrs Brown, who is unhappy about the change in her neighbour, Mrs White, who has returned to work after some years of looking after the home and children. Mrs Brown still does this and resents the implication that the world of work offers more interest than the domestic setting. The 'facts' of the matter are that Mrs Brown finds Mrs White 'unfriendly', and Mr Brown 'far too attentive' to her erstwhile friend. Students of social psychology could, if they wished, measure something of Mrs Brown's feelings and perhaps say that women who are placed in role-conflict situations like this one ('Do I work or stay at home?') suffer a loss of self-esteem. If one could repeat this study and perhaps do so showing levels of statistical significance, then one might have a finding indeed. Would it, however, reflect a fact? From what we have discussed so far, this would be a hasty conclusion to draw, because the 'facts' derive from a change to particular relationships involving the parties concerned. What we understand as friendship and as marriage are relationships which have distinct norms and values attached to them; in short, what people say and do within them is patterned in ways which we have discussed in terms of style and ritual. And should Mr and Mrs Brown finally have a stand-up argument over the matter, we might hear her say that she now realizes that, all the time she has been making herself available to help her husband, she should have been taking stock of her own needs. Perhaps she says that the problem is her relationship to Mr Brown, not to her neighbour. Once said, she realizes that she might have more in common with Mrs White than she thought; her feelings of jealousy evaporate, replaced by an awareness of the need to re-form her life along new lines, and to re-establish her identity.

This scenario ends, therefore, with politics, or ideology. The ideology lies in the unquestioned assumptions which underlie the marriage of the Browns, and the Whites too for that matter. Politics appears in the revelations of these assumptions in the Browns' arguments. Should this lead to insights on both of their parts, then they might feel that their marriage has to be placed upon a new footing. This footing is the framework within which their actions are repatterned, new rituals being enacted within which things appear differently, appear as new 'facts'. The interesting thing for us, as students of social relationships, is not the separation of fact from ritual from politics, but the changing relationship between these aspects of the Browns' life. To study these things we need to keep in mind such ideas as claim and counter-claim, appearances, multiple-group membership, social identity and ritual performances. In short, we need to study the giving, withholding and grasping of 'permission' in social life.

Arrivals and departures: staying with ambiguity

When I have been discussing a specific topic or examining the work of a particular author, I have deliberately tried to show how our understanding of that problem relies upon knowledge of other areas of social life. The book began with the claim that the study of groups presumes we know about individuals, and that the study of individuals assumes the contexts which group life provides. In the course of the chapters which followed, this claim has been used repeatedly to show that this is more than an idle point to make; once one starts looking to see how each topic depends upon our understanding of others, it becomes increasingly difficult to keep them apart. Appearances, the making of impressions and the degree to which we express ourselves bodily are tied up with group life. Claims to identity, external status characteristics, issues of gesture and deportment and the development of style involve multiple-group membership. The body, we have seen, is a social thing. From another standpoint the development of group norms depends upon the actions of individuals, so that we cannot understand the way in which things work out in real life without some grasp of the intentions and interpretations of the people involved.

Can we put all of these things together into a theory? If one means by this, can one show how each part fits together into a total explanation, the answer is 'advisable not to try'. The reason for this is that such an explanation would attempt to explain all social experience at a stroke, or in one penetrating stare. By doing this it would objectify and put on the table in front of us, as it were, the totality of the problem we want to study. And if that were possible, then we would have made social relationships into a 'thing' which could be inspected as a complete entity. However, one message from this book is that social relationships are not complete things; they are not unitary. They involve contradictions and ambiguities which spring from the fact that people have multiple engagements in life, say and do more (or less) than they intend, are open to misinterpretation by others and are more or less aware of the basis of their actions. They also live nearer to or further away from their hopes and dreams of what might be around the next corner, or what tomorrow might bring. In short, an essential part of social life is what might happen, or what might have happened, what could be done 'if', or what other people might think. This is not just a case for saying that life is uncertain, or not wholly predictable. It is an argument for seeing social relationships as being something like dramas, games, invitations and excursions which become something because someone else notices, cares, ignores, deliberately misrepresents or tries hard and fails. (Of course, not all social life appears like this; it can also be relatively clear cut and straightforward.)

The ambiguity in social relationships is not, therefore, accidental, by which I mean not 'by the way'. It comes from the fact that we are always having to act from some position or other, within some pattern of exchange, some place defined by our group membership. We cannot control this aspect, because we have to live it out, commit ourselves in some way. The information 'given off', the 'I' who acts, the 'performer' who makes claims through his or her behaviour, are concepts used to describe this aspect of the social individual. Sometimes the position from which we act becomes tangible to us only when others point out something about our behaviour, or when we cross the boundaries of other groups from which we review our past. My point is that people's actions and thoughts have an indefinable basis, and that it is no bad thing for the student to face this possibility.

Does this mean that we can explain some aspects of social interaction and not others? I think this is again to see the problem as if it were a thing which had a physical outline. In effect, when making the arguments in this book, I have been able to discuss some aspects of relationships because we relied upon others which we know from our experience as ordinary people. In turn, we could discuss appearances (using our tacit knowledge of groups), and later analyse group membership while relying upon our knowledge of ourselves as individuals who act with intent. In theorizing then, as in everyday life, we take different positions towards the problem. In so doing, that aspect which was tacit becomes the object, and that aspect which was previously the focus becomes part of the standpoint of thought. In each case there is always something that we cannot get in the forefront of our attention. Never escaping from this ambiguity, we are none the less able to use it and to see by it. When talking about groups, what we find out sheds further light on our understanding of the individual (e.g. social identity, perspectives and multiple groups); when talking about appearances we inform our understanding of groups (e.g. that groups may be established on the basis of interpretations). Our understanding of any given aspect of social life is deepened through its being reflected against another aspect which we assume. We progress in this form of enquiry by learning to bear with this ambiguity, not by trying to eradicate it through breaking the problem into separate pieces or by trying to build a monolithic theory.

One way in which social interaction can appear to be like facts – a process, a code, a causal chain – is when it is broken down into separate topics which each receive their own mini-explanation. For reasons which have been given above, the reader will see that this is an unsatisfactory approach. It tends towards a neat fit of mini-explanation on to mini-problem, so that what is there to be explained is increasingly defined by the theory which has been applied. In this book I have tried a different approach, the use of illustration and example. The effect of this is to bring to mind the different aspects of the problem together, as we know they are there in actuality. Describing people and their settings in a concrete way – how it would be in that place at that time – situates the problem so that we are more likely to see how the various aspects of social experience need to be considered together. If one talks only of 'individuals' but never of men and women, or of supervisors and workers, successful people and failures, then the way in which groups, claims and gestures appear together is less likely to be seen. There is much mileage, for the student, in getting used to thinking of social life in terms of example. It challenges the suppositions of researchers, provides one's own purchase on what can otherwise seem an abstract issue and refreshes one's view of what it is about social relationships which matters; it signifies what one wants to explain. It also gives you the confidence to know that the question which your example poses is relevant, is worth asking, even if (as may happen at the time) it is only being asked by yourself.

The ideas presented in this book help us to arrive at this position, where one stays with ambiguity rather than trying to avoid it or to extinguish it. This is not so much a conclusion about social interaction, as it is a point of departure for the student or lay person who wants to say something more about people in social relationships.

REFERENCES

Abercrombie, D. (1968). 'Paralanguage'. *British Journal of Disorders of Communication*, 3, 55–9.

Argyle, M. (1969). *Social Interaction*. London, Methuen.

(1973). *The Psychology of Interpersonal Behaviour*. (2nd edn), London, Penguin.

(1984). 'Some new developments in social skills training'. *Bulletin of the British Psychological Society*, 37, 405–10.

Argyle, M. and Dean, J. (1965). 'Eye-contact, distance and affiliation', *Sociometry*. 28, 289–304.

Argyle, M., Lalljee, M. and Cook, M. (1968). 'The effects of visibility on interaction in a dyad'. *Human Relations*, 21, 3–17.

Argyle, M., Salter, V., Nicholson, H., Williams, M. and Burgess, P. (1970). 'The communication of inferior and superior attitudes by verbal and non-verbal signals'. *British Journal of Social and Clinical Psychology*, 9, 222–31.

Bales, R.F. (1950). 'The analysis of small group interaction'. *American Sociological Review*, 15, 257–64.

(1958). 'Task roles and social roles in problem solving groups' in Maccoby, E.E., Newcomb, T.M. and Hartley, E.L. (eds.). *Readings in Social Psychology*. (3rd edn.), New York, Holt, Rinehart & Winston.

Bartol, K.M. and Martin, D.C. (1986). 'Women and men in task groups' in Ashmore, R.D. and del Boca, F.K. (eds.) *The Social Psychology of Female–Male Relations: A Critical Analysis of Central Concepts*. London, Academic Press.

Bateson, G. (1987). 'A theory of play and fantasy' in Bateson, G. *Steps to an Ecology of Mind*. London, Jason Aronson.

Beattie, G. (1983). *Talk: An Analysis of Speech and Non-verbal Behaviour in Conversation*. Milton Keynes, Open University Press.

Berger, P., Berger, B. and Kellner, H. (1974). *The Homeless Mind: Modernization and Consciousness*. Harmondsworth, Penguin.

Berscheid, E. and Walster, E. (1974). 'Physical attractiveness' in Berkowitz, L. (ed.). *Advances in experimental social psychology* (vol. 7). New York, Academic Press: 158–216.

Bion, W.I. (1961). *Experiences in Groups*. London, Tavistock.

Birdwhistell, R. (1971). *Kinesics and Context: Essays on Body-motion Communication*. London, Allen Lane.

Boski, P. and Rudmin, F. (1989). 'Ichheiser's theories of personality and person perception: a classic that still inspires'. *Journal for the Theory of Social Behaviour*, 19, 263–96.

Branthwaite, A. and Jones, J.E. (1975). 'Fairness and discrimination: English versus Welsh'. *European Journal of Social Psychology*, 5, 323–38.

Breed, G. (1972). 'The effect of intimacy: reciprocity or retreat?' *British Journal of Social and Clinical Psychology*, 11, 135–42.

Bugental, D.E., Kaswan, J.W. and Love, L.R. (1970). 'Perception of contradictory meanings conveyed by verbal and non-verbal channels'. *Journal of Personality and Social Psychology*, 16, 647–55.

Bull, P. (1983). *Body movement and interpersonal communication*. London, Wiley.

Burke, P.J. (1973). 'The development of task and social-emotional role differentiation' in Ofshe, R.J. *Interpersonal Behavior in Small Groups*. New York, Prentice-Hall.

Clarke, J., Hall, S., Jefferson, T. and Roberts, B. (1976). 'Subcultures, cultures and class' in Hall, S. and Jefferson, T. (eds.) *Resistance Through Rituals*, London, Hutchinson.

Coser, R.L. (1975). 'The complexity of roles as a seedbed of individual autonomy' in Coser, L.A. (ed.). *The Idea of Social Structure: papers in honor of Robert K. Merton*. New York, Harcourt Brace Jovanavich.

Dean, L.M., Willis, F.N. and Hewitt, J. (1975). 'Initial interaction distance among individuals equal and unequal in military rank'. *Journal of Personality and Social Psychology*, 32, 294–9.

Douglas, M. (1971). 'Do dogs laugh? A Cross-cultural Approach to Body Symbolism'. *Journal of Psychosomatic Research*, 15, 387–90.

(1973). *Natural Symbols: Explorations in Cosmology*. Harmondsworth, Penguin.

Duncan, S. (1969). 'Non-verbal communication'. *Psychological Bulletin*, 72, 118–37.

Edinger, J.A. and Patterson, M.L. (1983). 'Non-verbal involvement and social control'. *Psychological Bulletin*, 93, 30–56.

Efron, D. (1972). *Gesture, Race and Culture*. The Hague, Mouton.

Eibl-Eibesfeldt, I. (1972). 'Similarities and differences between cultures in expressive movements' in Hinde, R.A. (ed.) *Nonverbal Communication*. Cambridge, Cambridge University Press.

(1979). 'Universals in human expressive behaviour' in Wolfgang, A. (ed.). *Nonverbal Behavior: applications and cultural implications*. New York, Academic Press.

Ekman, P. (1977). 'Biological and cultural contributions to body and facial movement' in Blacking, J. (ed.). *The Anthropology of the Body*. London, Academic Press.

Ekman, P. and Friesen, W.V. (1969a). 'The repertoire of nonverbal behavior: categories, origins, usage, and coding. *Semiotica*, 1, 49–98.

(1969b). 'Non-verbal leakage and clues to deception'. *Psychiatry*, 32, 88–105.

(1971). 'Constants across cultures in the face and emotion'. *Journal of Personality and Social Psychology*, 17, 124–9.

Ellis, R. and Whittington, D. (1981). *A Guide to Social Skills Training*. London, Croom Helm.

Feiffer, J. (1972). *Carnal Knowledge*. Harmondsworth, Penguin.

Fisher, J.D., Rytting, M. and Heslin, J. (1976). 'Hands touching hands: affective and evaluative effects of interpersonal touch'. *Sociometry*, 39, 416–21.

Geertz, H. (1959). 'The vocabulary of emotion: a study of Javanese socialisation process'. *Psychiatry*, 22, 225–37.

Goffman, E. (1961). *Encounters: Two Studies in the Sociology of Interaction*. Indianapolis, Bobbs-Merrill.

(1963). *Stigma: Notes on the Management of Spoiled Identity*. Englewood Cliffs, N.J., Prentice-Hall.

(1970). *Strategic Interaction*. Oxford, Blackwell.

(1971). *The Presentation of Self in Everyday Life*. Harmondsworth, Penguin.

(1972). *Interaction Ritual: Essays on Face-to-face Behaviour*. Harmondsworth, Penguin.

(1975). *Frame Analysis: An Essay on the Organization of Experience*, Harmondsworth, Penguin.

Guetzkow, H. and Simon, H.A. (1955) 'The impact of certain communication nets upon organization and performance in task-oriented groups'. *Management Science*, 1, 233–50.

Hall, J.A. (1978). 'Gender effects in decoding nonverbal cues'. *Psychological Bulletin*, 85, 845–57.

Harré, R. and Secord, P.F. (1972). *The Explanation of Social Behaviour*. Oxford, Blackwell.

Hebdige, D. (1979). *Subculture: The Meaning of Style*. London, Methuen.

Heider, F. (1958). *The Psychology of Interpersonal Relations*. London, Wiley.

Henley, N.M. (1977). *Body politics: Power, Sex and Nonverbal Communication*. New York, Simon & Schuster.

Hinde, R.A. (ed.) (1972). *Nonverbal Communication*. Cambridge, Cambridge University Press.

Homans, G.C. (1951). *The Human Group*. London, Routledge & Kegan Paul.

Ichheiser, G. (1933). 'Das Koennen, die Bedingungen des Koennens, und das Erlebnis des Koennens. *Z. angew. Psychol.*, 44, 367–78.

(1949). 'Misunderstandings in human relations'. *American Journal of Sociology*, 55, 2, Whole Part 2.

(1970). *Appearances and Realities*. San Francisco, Jossey-Bass.

Jenni, D.A. and Jenni, M.A. (1976). 'Carrying behavior in humans: analyses of sex differences'. *Science*, 194, 859–60.

Jennings H.H. (1950). *Leadership and Isolation* (2nd edn). New York, Longmans, Green.

Jones, E.E., Davis, K.E. and Gergen, K.L. (1961). 'Role playing variations and their informational value for person perception'. *Journal of Abnormal and Social Psychology*, 63, 302–10.

Jones, E.E. and de Charms, R. (1958). 'Changes in social perception as a function of the personal relevance of behaviour' in Maccoby, E.E., Newcomb, T.M. and Hartley, E.L. (eds.) *Readings in Social Psychology* (3rd edn). New York, Holt, Rinehart & Winston.

Jourard, S. (1966). 'An exploratory study of body accessibility.' *British Journal of Social and Clinical Psychology*, 5, 221–31.

Kanter, R.M. (1977). 'Some effects of proportions on group life: skewed sex ratios and responses to token women'. *American Journal of Sociology*, 82, 965–90.

Kendon, A. (1967). 'Some functions of gaze in social interaction'. *Acta Psychologica*, 26, 1–47.

— (1975). 'Some functions of the face in a kissing round'. *Semiotica*, 15, 299–334.

Kleinke, C.L. (1986). 'Gaze and eye contact: a research review'. *Psychological Bulletin*, 100, 78–100.

Kleinke, C.L., Bustos, A.A., Meeker, F.B. and Staneski, R.A. (1973). 'Effects of self-attributed and other-attributed gaze on interpersonal evaluations between males and females'. *Journal of Experimental Social Psychology*, 9, 154–63.

LaFrance, M. and Mayo, C. (1976). 'Racial differences in gaze behavior during conversations: two systematic observational studies'. *Journal of Personality and Social Psychology*, 33, 547–52.

Langer, S.K. (1957). *Philosophy in a New Key: A Study in the Symbolism of Reason, Rite and Art* (3rd edn). Cambridge, Mass: Harvard University Press.

Laver, J. and Hutcheson, S. (eds.) (1972). *Communication in Face-to-face Interaction*. Harmondsworth, Penguin.

Leavitt, H.J. (1951). 'Some effects of certain communication patterns on group performance'. *Journal of Abnormal and Social Psychology*, 46, 38–50.

Leik, R.K. (1963). 'Instrumentality and emotionality in family interaction'. *Sociometry*, 26, 131–45.

Lessing, D. (1972). *The Golden Notebook* (rev.edn). London, Michael Joseph.

Marsh, P., Rosser, E. and Harré, R. (1978). *The Rules of Disorder*. London, Routledge & Kegan Paul.

Mauss, M. (1972). 'Techniques of the body'. *Economy and Society*, 2, 70–88.

Mead, G.H. (1934). *Mind, Self and Society*. Chicago, University of Chicago Press.

Mead, M. (1942). 'Balinese character'. In Bateson, G. and Mead, M. *Balinese Character: A Photographic Analysis*. Special publication of the New York Academy of Sciences, Vol. II.

Moore, S.F. and Myerhoff, B.G. (eds.) (1977). *Secular Ritual*. Amsterdam, Van Gorcum.

Moreland, R.L. and Levine, J.M. (1988). 'Group dynamics over time: development and socialization in small groups' in McGrath, J.E. (ed.) *The Social Psychology of Time: New Perspectives*. London, Sage.

Morris, J. (1972). 'Three aspects of the person in social life' in Ruddock, R. (ed.) *Six Approaches to the Person*. London, Routledge & Kegan Paul.

Moscovici, S. and Paichelier, G. (1978). 'Social comparison and social recognition: two complementary processes of identification' in Tajfel, H. (ed.) *Differentiation Between Social Groups: Studies in the Social Psychology of Intergroup Relations*. London, Academic Press.

Noller, P. (1980). 'Misunderstandings in marital communication: a study of couples' nonverbal communication'. *Journal of Personality and Social Psychology*, 39, 1135–48.

Patterson, M.L.A. (1982). 'A sequential functional model of non-verbal exchange'. *Psychological Review*, 89, 231–49.

Polanyi, M. (1967). *The Tacit Dimension*. London, Routledge & Kegan Paul.

Radley, A. (1978). 'Deliberation and awareness in personal conduct'. *Journal of Phenomenological Psychology*, 8, 181–202.

— (1985). 'From courtesy to strategy: some old developments in social skills training': *Bulletin of the British Psychological Society*, 38, 209–11.

Robinson, M. (1984). *Groups*. Chichester, Wiley.

Rose, N. (1989). 'Psychology as a "social" science'. In I. Parker and J. Shotter (eds.) *Deconstructing Social Psychology*, London: Routledge.

Rosenthal, R. and DePaulo, B.M. (1979). 'Sex differences in accommodation in non-verbal communication' in Rosenthal, R. (ed.) *Skill in Non-Verbal Communication*. Cambridge, Mass., Oelgeschlager, Gunn and Hain.

Rosenthal, R. and Jacobson, L. (1966). 'Teachers' expectancies. Determinants of pupils' I.Q. gains'. *Psychological Reports*, 19, 115–18.

Schank, R.C. and Abelson, R.P. (1977). *Scripts, Plans, Goals, and Understanding: An Inquiry into Human Knowledge Structures*. Hillsdale, N.J., Erlbaum.

Scheflen, A.E. (1965). 'Quasi-courtship behavior in psychotherapy'. *Psychiatry*, 28, 245–57.

(1972). *Body Language and Social Order*. Englewood Cliffs, N.J., Prentice-Hall.

(1979). 'On communicational processes' in Wolfgang, A. (ed.) *Nonverbal Behavior: Applications and Cultural Implications*. London, Academic Press.

Schneider, D.J., Hastorf, A.H. and Ellsworth, P.C. (1979). *Person Perception* (2nd edn). Reading, Mass., Addison-Wesley.

Scott, R.A. (1969). *The Making of Blind Men: A Study of Adult Socialization*. New York, Russell Sage Foundation.

Shaw, M.E. and Shaw, L.M. (1962). 'Some effects of sociometric grouping upon learning in a second grade classroom'. *Journal of Social Psychology*, 57, 453–8.

Sherif, M. (1966). *Group Conflict and Cooperation: Their Social Psychology*. London, Routledge & Kegan Paul.

Shibutani, T. (1955). 'Reference groups as perspectives'. *American Journal of Sociology*, 60, 562–70.

Simmel, G. (1955). *Conflict and The Web of Group Affiliations*. New York, Free Press.

(1965). 'The significance of numbers for social life' in Hare, A.P., Borgatta, E.F. and Bales, R.F. (eds.) *Small Groups: Studies in Social Interaction*. New York, Knopf.

Skevington, S. (1981). 'Intergroup relations and nursing'. *European Journal of Social Psychology*, 11, 43–59.

Smail, D. (1984). *Illusion and Reality: The Meaning of Anxiety*. London, Dent.

Sommer, R. (1965). 'Further studies of small-group ecology'. *Sociometry*, 28, 337–48.

Soucie, R. (1979). 'Common misconceptions about nonverbal communication: implications for training' in Wolfgang, A. (ed.) *Nonverbal Behaviour: Applications and Cultural Implications*. London, Academic Press.

Strodtbeck, F.L., James, R.M. and Hawkins, C. (1957). 'Social status in jury deliberations'. *American Sociological Review*, 22, 713–19.

Tolstoy, L.N. (1954). *Anna Karenin* (trans. Rosemary Edmonds). Harmondsworth, Penguin.

Trower, P., Bryant, B. and Argyle, M. (1978). *Social Skills and Mental Health*. London, Methuen.

Turner, J.C. (1987). *Rediscovering the Social Group*. Oxford, Blackwell.

Turner, T.S. (1977). 'Transformation, hierarchy and transcendence: a reformulation of Van Gennep's model of the structure of rites de passage' in Moore, S.F. and Myerhoff, B.G. (eds.) *Secular Ritual*. Amsterdam, Van Gorcum.

Vygotsky, L.S. (1962). *Thought and Language*. Cambridge, Mass., MIT Press.

(1976). 'Play and its role in the mental development of the child' in Bruner, J.S.,

Jolly, A. and Sylva, K. (eds.) *Play: its role in development and evolution.* Harmondsworth, Penguin.

Watzlawick, P., Beavin, J.H. and Jackson, D.D. (1967). *Pragmatics of Human Communication.* New York, Norton.

Whyte, W.F. (1981). *Street Corner Society* (3rd edn). Chicago, University of Chicago Press.

Wiener, M., Devoe, S., Rubinow, S. and Geller, J. (1972). 'Nonverbal behavior and nonverbal communication'. *Psychological Review,* 79, 185–214.

Wildeblood, J. (1973). *The Polite World: A Guide to the Deportment of the English in Former Times.* London, Davis-Poynter.

Wilkinson, J. and Canter, S. (1982). *Social Skills Training Manual.* London, Wiley.

Willis, P.E. (1975). 'The expressive style of a motor-bike culture' in Benthall, J. and Polhemus, T. (eds.) *The Body as a Medium of Expression.* London, Allen Lane.

Wilson, S. (1978). *Informal Groups: An Introduction.* Englewood Cliffs, NJ, Prentice-Hall.

Winnicott, D.W. (1971). *Playing and Reality.* London, Tavistock.

Zelditch, M. (1956). 'Role differentiation in the nuclear family' in Parsons, T. and Bales, R.F. (eds.) *Family Socialization and Interaction Process.* London, Routledge & Kegan Paul.

AUTHOR INDEX

SUBJECT INDEX